D1006893

Harriet Tubman

Harriet Tubman

Kem Knapp Sawyer

DK PUBLISHING

LONDON, NEW YORK, MUNICH,
MELBOURNE, AND DELHI

Editor : Beth Landis Hester
Publishing Director : Beth Sutinis
Designer : Mark Johnson Davies
Managing Art Editor : Michelle Baxter
Production Controller : Erika Pepe
DTP Coordinator : Kathy Farias
Photo Research : Anne Burns Images

First American Edition, 2010

10 11 12 13 14 10 9 8 7 6 5 4 3 2 1
Published in the United States
by DK Publishing
375 Hudson Street
New York, New York 10014

Copyright © 2010 DK Publishing
Text copyright © 2010 Kem Knapp Sawyer
All rights reserved under International and
Pan-American Copyright Conventions. No
part of this publication may be reproduced,
stored in a retrieval system, or transmitted
in any form or by any means, electronic,
mechanical, photocopying, recording,
or otherwise, without the prior written
permission of the copyright owner.

DK books are available at special discounts
when purchased in bulk for sales promotions,
premiums, fund-raising,
or educational use. For details, contact:

DK Publishing Special Markets
375 Hudson Street
New York, New York 10014
SpecialSales@dk.com

A catalog record for this book is available
from the Library of Congress.

ISBN 978-0-7566-5806-9 (Paperback)
ISBN 978-0-7566-5807-6 (Hardcover)

Printed and bound in China
by South China Printing Co., Ltd.

Discover more at
www.dk.com

Contents

chapter **1**

One More Soul Is Safe

Joe Bailey traveled by night, often in disguise. Slave catchers were searching for him. Eager to claim a reward, they could be anywhere. Joe had to move carefully so as not to get caught. He wanted to be free and he was willing to risk his life for it. But one wrong move and his plan would fail.

The young man was not alone. He had the best of guides: Harriet Tubman. She too had been a slave in Maryland. Like Joe, she had left behind everything that was familiar. She had dared to leave, to go north and start a new life. She had found freedom—later returning to the place she had

Fugitive slaves often traveled by night, hiding in tall grasses and the woods by day.

once called home, eager to lead others out of slavery. This time she agreed to take Joe, his brother William, their friend Peter, and a woman named Eliza. They would sleep in a potato field or on a bed of moss, deep in the woods.

Fugitive slaves lived in fear of being captured by slave catchers.

Sometimes they found refuge in safe houses belonging to free African-Americans or white abolitionists who sympathized with their cause.

But as soon as they reached the Delaware River on the state border, they knew there would be trouble. Police stood guard on the bridge, on the lookout for fugitives. Harriet sent word to her friend on the other side—a Quaker named Thomas Garrett who lived in the town of Wilmington. Thomas enlisted the help of bricklayers working on a construction project near the entrance to the bridge.

At the end of the day the workmen prepared to cross the bridge and return home. They hid the fugitives in their wagon. Lying in a secret compartment beneath the floor of the wagon, Joe could hear the workers singing and shouting. The guards were not the least suspicious. They let the wagon pass.

Harriet led the fugitives to Philadelphia and then took them by train to New York City. Joe was cold and hungry, but that mattered little now that he had escaped his master.

Harriet brought the group to the antislavery office where they thought they would have cause to celebrate. But the news

The Niagara Falls Suspension Bridge, completed in 1855, connected New York State and Ontario, Canada. It spanned 825 ft (251 m) and allowed for the passage of both wagons and trains.

Joe heard was unexpected—the man who had been his master was now offering a $1,500 reward for his capture. Joe could still be arrested even in New York; his best hope lay in Canada. Three hundred miles separated him from freedom.

Once again Harriet and her party boarded the train. As they rode across the rolling hills of New York State Joe was silent. Harriet tried to lift his spirits, but Joe remained fearful. The group arrived safely at the Canadian border and prepared to cross the Niagara River on the suspension bridge that linked the United States to Canada.

Harriet sang:

"I'm on the way to Canada,
That cold and dreary land. . . .

Farewell, old Master, don't think hard of me,

I'm traveling on to Canada, where all the slaves are free."

Others on the train joined in the song, but Joe would not. He held his head in his hands.

Harriet's Stories

Harriet was never taught to read or write, but she was a wonderful storyteller. Her audience always listened attentively—at once charmed by her manner and in awe of her courage and her optimism. Joe's flight to freedom was one of her stories.

From the bridge the passengers could hear the roar of the rushing water and the cry of the seagulls. They could see white sheets of ice, water pounding on the rock, and glistening rays of light. Their faces were wet from the mist that sprayed through the open window. For many fugitives this first view of the magnificent falls was a joyful moment—the landmark a symbol of the freedom they had struggled to obtain. But Joe kept his head down and said nothing. He still thought he could be captured.

Once they passed the center of the bridge Harriet pointed to the giant falls shaped like a horseshoe and shook Joe by the shoulder. "You're a free man!" she yelled. Joe looked up at Harriet and through the window at the falls. Now he was safe. He shouted out in song:

"Oh, go and carry the news
One more soul is safe."

The train stopped on Canadian soil. After the conductor climbed down from the train, Joe was the first to follow.

chapter 2

A Sweet Gum Cradle

The first white settlers landed on Maryland's shores in 1634. Within a few years black men and women had also arrived. They had been captured in Africa, taken onto a ship, and transported to America where they were treated like indentured servants—working for their master for several years before being released. By the end of the 17th century,

Although the enslaved family in this photograph spans five generations, slaves had no guarantee that their families would remain together.

more than 3,000 Africans were living in the Chesapeake Bay region of Maryland. However they were no longer set free after a prescribed number of years, but remained in slavery, and their children too became slaves. Any child born to an enslaved woman would also be enslaved, even if the father were not.

The work slaves had to perform was difficult—it could also be demeaning, tedious, and strenuous. Slaves were often whipped and beaten.

Enslavers relied on a whip—as well as the threat of auction—to maintain discipline.

They were treated by their enslavers not as people, but as property, or "chattel." For many, the hardest burden to bear was the fear that came with not knowing what the future held. At any moment the enslaver could exercise his right to sell the men, women, and children who lived on his land.

Atthow Pattison was a Marylander who had fought in the Revolutionary War. His family had lived in Dorchester County on the Eastern Shore of

Some slave ships carried as many as 600 Africans. Men, women, and children were forced to lie side by side in the hull, with no room to sit or stand.

Maryland, near the Chesapeake Bay, for more than a century. The Pattisons had accumulated 265 acres of land—marsh, fields, and forest. Much of the land remained as it had always been—unspoiled by inhabitants. Sea grass and cattails lined the horizon. Underfoot the ground was damp and often muddy. Geese and ducks made their home along the swamp. The pine forest provided a haven for deer and fox, raccoons and muskrats. Farther inland cornfields had replaced the tobacco farms.

Although residents of the Eastern Shore had petitioned the Maryland House of Delegates to abolish slavery in 1785, Atthow, like many landowners, was unperturbed and kept several

The marsh along the Blackwater River is home to bald eagles and osprey as well as ducks and geese.

ABOLISH

To abolish a practice, such as slavery, is to outlaw or bring an end to it.

slaves to manage his property. (The average number of slaves owned by a slaveholder was 11.) One of the slaves Atthow had purchased was a woman named Modesty. It is likely that Modesty came from Ghana in West Africa and that she was of Ashanti heritage.

The Ashanti were known for their physical strength and endurance, and a deep spirituality. They mined gold and were also successful farmers, growing yams, cassava, and plantains. Women were highly respected and often took leadership roles. Thousands of Ashanti were captured and sold as part of the triangular trade between Europe, Africa, and the New World. Many were brought to the Eastern Shore on a slave ship and sold at the dock or in slave markets in Oxford or Cambridge, Maryland.

By 1810, almost two million people of African descent were enslaved in

Triangular trade

European sea captains traveled to Africa to exchange manufactured goods, guns, and ammunition for Africans, usually from conquered tribes. Men, women, and children were enslaved and transported to the New World. There they were sold—or traded for sugar, tobacco, rice, rum, or cotton— goods that were then taken back to Europe.

the New World—18,000 were living in Maryland, and 5,000 of them in Dorchester County. But

Published in a British newspaper, this wood engraving of the auctioning of an African-American woman helped raise awareness of the cruelty of the institution.

not all Marylanders of African descent were slaves; early on, some Africans had come to the New World as explorers or sailors—and their descendants were now free.

The first protests from abolitionists (those who argued for abolishing slavery) came soon after the first slaves arrived in the New World. On April 18, 1688, the Mennonites, a Protestant group who had come from Switzerland and the Netherlands, signed the first antislavery resolution in North America. The Quakers and the Methodists followed suit. In 1793, the Emancipation Act of Upper Canada limited the terms slaves had to serve and prohibited bringing new slaves into the country. Britain put an end to the slave trade in 1807—due, in large part, to the determination and

EMANCIPATION

The act of emancipation grants freedom and political rights to individuals who have been denied them.

hard work of William Wilberforce, a member of the British Parliament. And, on January 1, 1808, the United States also ended the importation of slaves.

Although there was a ban on the slave trade, slavery itself was not abolished. Those who were born into slavery would remain enslaved—and their children would also be denied freedom.

Records of births, marriages, and deaths were not always accurately recorded—if at all—so the lives and histories of enslaved people may not be well documented. Modesty, the

Before enslaved Africans were sold or auctioned, they were held in pens like these in Alexandria, Virginia, within view of the nation's capital.

Slaves young and old were subjected to cruel treatment. Yet some children found time to play.

Ashanti slave, gave birth to a daughter, Harriet, between 1785 and 1789—the exact date has not been determined. She was called Rittia by the Pattisons and Rit by her family. Little is known about Rit's father. Historians have speculated that he might have been Atthow, Modesty's master, but there is no evidence or proof.

Atthow Pattison, in a will written in 1791, indicated that his granddaughter Mary Pattison would inherit Rittia—and any children she might have. The will also provided for Rit's manumission at the age of 45. Any children born to Rit would obtain their freedom when they turned 45.

Mary was only a year or two older than Rit—the two had lived in the same household since they were little girls. They may have spent time together and enjoyed each other's company, but the inequality of the relationship would never be forgotten nor taken lightly. Mary would always have the upper hand. And, when Atthow died in 1797, Mary became Rit's enslaver.

MANUMISSION

Manumission is the act of granting freedom to a slave.

In 1800, Mary wed Joseph Brodess, a farmer who lived close by in Bucktown, also in Dorchester County.

FOREMAN

A foreman takes charge of a work crew.

Their son Edward was born the following year. Edward was only one year old when his father died. In 1803 the young widow married Anthony Thompson, a widower who owned land 10 miles (16 km) to the west near the Blackwater River. Mary and her son, as well as Rit and four slaves who had belonged to her husband, moved onto Anthony's farm. There Rit first met Ben Ross, a slave who was the foreman for

Unlike the grand plantation houses where their enslavers lived, slaves were housed in relatively crude cottages, often grouped together in a kind of village.

Anthony. (Of Ben's heritage nothing is known.) Ben and Rit fell in love and, within a few years, the two were married and moved to a cabin on the Thompson property.

Mary Thompson died while her son Edward was still a child. Anthony Thompson became his stepson's guardian and would be responsible for Rit until Edward, who had legally inherited her, became an adult. Although Rit did some work for Anthony, he would also hire her out—saving her pay to give to Edward when he came of age.

When Edward Brodess reached adulthood he would claim not only Rit, but her children as well. And there would be several born before Edward turned 21: Ben and Rit's first child, Linah, was born in or around 1808. Two more daughters followed: Mariah Ritty in 1811 and Soph in 1813. Robert, the first son, was born three years later.

Harriet Tubman was the fifth child born to Rit and Ben. Her parents named her Araminta, and she was called Minty. (Later, when she was married, she changed

This 1839 record of people enslaved by Anthony Thompson lists Ben (Harriet Tubman's father) and also refers to his "wife & children belonging to Edward Brodess."

her name to Harriet.) Like many slaves, she did not know her birthday or the year of her birth. As an adult, she would often say she was born in 1825. Her death certificate, however, states that she was born in 1815, and her gravestone bears the year 1820.

Only recently has it been determined that Harriet was born in 1822. A record of a two-dollar payment from Anthony Thompson to a midwife for help in delivering a baby born to Rit is now believed to be connected to Harriet's birth.

Sweet Gum Trees

Sweet gum trees grow as high as 60 or 70 feet (18–21 m) on the Eastern Shore. Harriet learned to recognize the large leaves—star-shaped with five or seven points. Beautiful furniture and boxes were frequently made from the trunk or limbs, and the gum underneath the bark was used in medicines.

This transaction took place on March 15, 1822, which would indicate that the baby was born in February or March.

Years later Harriet remembered lying in a cradle carved from the hollow trunk of a sweet gum tree. Young ladies from "the big house" where the Thompsons lived would pick her up from the cradle, gently throw her up into the air, and catch her. For Harriet the cradle her father built would always be a precious memory connecting her to her roots on the Eastern Shore.

chapter 3
A Blow to the Head

The lives of the Ross family would be intertwined with the families of Anthony Thompson and Edward Brodess for many years. When Edward reached the age of 21, he did not immediately move into his own home. Rit and her young children remained with the Thompsons, while the older children may have been hired out. Meanwhile, four more children were born to Rit and Ben: three sons—Ben, Henry, and Moses—and a daughter named Rachel.

In 1824, at the age of 23, Edward married Eliza Ann Keene and moved with his new wife to Bucktown, into a house built on the family property.

This map of Dorchester County shows plantations near Bucktown, including the Brodess and Thompson farms.

Within the next few years (no clear date has been established) Rit moved onto the Brodess farm. Her children came with her, since they too belonged to Edward. But Ben had to remain behind with Anthony Thompson. The separation was difficult for the family. Even more wrenching was the sale of Harriet's older sister Mariah. At the age of 16, she was sold to slaveholders "down south," where conditions were thought to be much worse than in Maryland. She left Maryland, never to return again—and never to be reunited with her family.

Harriet Tubman Marker in Bucktown

This plaque on Greenbriar Road outside Bucktown marks the reputed place of Harriet Tubman's birth, once home to Edward Brodess. Given that it has now been determined that Harriet was born in 1822, historians agree that she would have been born on land in Peter's Neck belonging to Anthony Thompson. However, it is here in Bucktown that she would have spent much of her childhood.

No slave could escape the fear of being sold. By law, enslavers could auction or sell their slaves whenever they wanted. Some owners gave little thought to such a sale; others exercised their "right" only as a last resort. If their crops failed or an economic downturn got the better of them, they might see selling a slave as the only way to bring

in extra money. Edward's finances were precarious—
he probably sold Mariah to reduce his debt.

Once Rit and her children moved to Bucktown, Rit
worked as a cook in "the big house"—where Edward and
Eliza Brodess lived. The older children also had to work.
That left little Harriet to care for the younger ones—
a responsibility she took on when she was only four years
old. Harriet liked to pretend her baby brother was a "pig in
a bag." Turning him upside down (no doubt holding him by
the bottom of his long dress), she would swing him around.
If Rit had to work late, Harriet often found herself at her
wit's end. She'd cut off a chunk of pork, toast it in the coals,
and feed it to her baby brother. Once he went to sleep with
the piece of meat hanging out of his mouth. Rit checked on

As a child, Harriet would cross the Blackwater River on a footbridge. She used this shortcut to travel from her mother's quarters on the Brodess farm to her father's cabin on Anthony Thompson's property.

The farm on this property in Bucktown was home to Edward Brodess and his wife Eliza.

him as soon as she returned, but she mistook the pork for his tongue and thought her baby boy had died. What a relief to find the chunk of pork!

Harriet was not yet eight years old when Edward hired her out to a neighbor, James Cook, and his wife, who was a weaver. This was a common practice on the Eastern Shore—for children as well as adults. Employers sometimes provided room and board and they might pay the slave owner as much as $120 for a year's work, a substantial sum at the time.

James Cook carried Harriet on horseback the 10 miles (16 km) to his house. She was to be trained as a weaver, but she was also told to check the muskrat traps. (Muskrats are small furry animals who live in the marsh.) Expectations were high: Even when sick with measles and running a fever, Harriet had to wade through the wetlands to get the job done. She missed her family and, at night, cried herself to sleep as she lay on the kitchen floor in front of the fireplace. Harriet

Muskrats build homes of sticks and mud, often 3 feet (1 m) in diameter. Their dwellings remain dry although the entrance is underwater.

remained with the Cooks for two years, but had little success in learning to weave.

Harriet was soon hired out again, this time to do housework and care for a baby. She was taught to call the mistress of the house "Miss Susan," as was the custom for slaves. Miss Susan made her watch over the baby at night, rocking the cradle without pausing to rest. Harriet hardly ever slept. If she did drift off and the baby cried, Miss Susan whipped her soundly.

During the day Harriet was told to sweep the carpet and dust the furniture. Unfortunately, her housekeeping skills were not up to Miss Susan's standards. Once Harriet tried four times—sweeping vigorously and then dusting as soon as she put the broom down. But each time Miss Susan found a layer of dust on the furniture and after each failed attempt she gave Harriet a beating.

On the fifth try, Susan's sister Emily intervened. Emily explained to Harriet

"I grew up neglected like a weed, ignorant of liberty, having no experience of it."

–Harriet to Benjamin Drew

that when she swept the dust flew into the air. She needed to let the dust settle before she tried to remove it. Harriet did as she was told and the day ended without another whipping.

Harriet's sweet tooth sometimes got her into trouble. One morning she couldn't help "stealing" a lump of sugar from the sugar bowl. Her mistress caught sight of her and chased after her. Harriet kept running—all the way to the pigpen. She climbed inside, joining a sow and 10 little piglets. She wouldn't have minded eating the potato peelings, but the sow wanted to make sure there was enough food for her piglets and refused to share. Harriet hid from Friday to Tuesday, but she was so hungry she returned to the house. She was whipped—this time by her master. Harriet's body would be covered with

In this 1834 woodcut, African-American children serve a meal to a white family. Slaves as young as five were put to work.

The injury that caused Harriet's narcolepsy may have occurred here in this Bucktown store (which is still standing) or in the immediate vicinity.

cuts and bruises— some of the scars would remain for the rest of her life.

Much to her relief, Harriet was soon sent home and hired out to a neighboring farmer. While she was at the general store on the road next to the Brodess property, she found herself in the middle of a dispute between an overseer and a young slave. The overseer was angry that the slave had come to the store without permission and he told Harriet to assist him in tying the slave's hands. Harriet refused. As the slave tried to escape, Harriet stood blocking the doorway so the overseer could not follow him. The overseer grabbed an iron weight and threw it at the fugitive. It missed its target, but hit Harriet, slicing the shawl she was wearing and drawing blood from her head. Harriet fell to the ground and had to be carried home.

The following morning she still felt faint. She could hardly move and stayed inside. After two days of rest,

OVERSEER

An overseer supervises the workers on a farm or plantation.

her employer forced her to return to the fields—even though she was still in pain and her head continued to bleed. It took months for the wound to heal.

The injury would have long-term consequences. Harriet suffered from headaches for much of her life, as well as narcolepsy—she fell asleep at inopportune moments, when she least expected to. She would awake moments later scarcely knowing what had happened.

Soon after receiving this blow, Harriet started to have vivid dreams—many of them she believed were messages from God. She could not always interpret them, but she was confident that one day their meaning would become clear. Harriet felt a spiritual connection that would become deeper as years passed. "I was always talking to the Lord," she said.

Nat Turner Rebellion

Nat Turner (1800–1831) was born a slave in Southampton County, Virginia. In August 1831, following what he believed to be "signs in the heavens," he led a slave revolt resulting in the deaths of more than 55 white people. Turner was captured, tried, and hanged; 55 other slaves were also executed. After the uprising, African-Americans in Virginia (both enslaved and free) were allowed fewer rights than ever before.

NARCOLEPSY

A person with narcolepsy experiences periods of extreme drowsiness during the day and also falls asleep unexpectedly.

chapter **4**

Hired Out

Anthony Thompson had hired Harriet's father, Ben, out to work for John Stewart, the owner of a prosperous lumber business on the Eastern Shore. Ben inspected the timber and took charge of cutting it as well as hauling it to the Baltimore shipyards. Not long after Harriet's head injury, Ben convinced Edward Brodess to let Harriet assist him in the timber business. Harriet

The timber industry provided an important source of wealth for Maryland landowners, such as John Stewart, Ben's employer.

was hired out for $50 or $60 a year—that sum would go to Edward Brodess. But any additional money she earned she could keep. (In one year she saved $40, enough to buy a pair of steers.)

Harriet worked for her father and on neighboring farms. As a young girl, she had always been fit; now that she was a teenager she had grown more muscular and she preferred to work outdoors, rather than inside. Harriet's physical strength was astonishing,

African-American Religious Practices

African-Americans on the Eastern Shore inherited the traditional African reverence for nature, and were also influenced by various Christian denominations. (Many of Maryland's white families belonged to Anglican, Episcopal, Catholic, or Methodist churches.) Some slaveholders encouraged their slaves to attend church services led by white clergy, but would not allow them to organize their own churches. Free blacks, on the other hand, started to form African Methodist Episcopal churches at the beginning of the 19th century.

all the more so given that she was only 5 feet (1.5 m) tall. She could lift barrels of grain, drive oxen, plow fields, cart manure, and chop wood—jobs often reserved for men. She also tended to menial tasks such as husking corn and preparing the wheat for the mill.

Harriet was still a dreamer. Often, while at work, she would have visions of herself "flying over fields and towns, and rivers and mountains, looking down upon them 'like a bird,' and reaching at last a great fence, or sometimes a river." She saw ladies dressed in white—they put out their arms and pulled

> *"She used to dream of flying over fields and towns, and rivers and mountains."*
>
> –Franklin Sanborn, about Harriet Tubman

her across the river—a vision she had more than once. These recurring dreams must have given her hope that one day freedom would be hers. They must have also provided her with the inner strength to tackle the daunting physical challenges she faced.

Although Harriet did not attend church regularly, her religious faith grew stronger. Ben and Rit would have told their children

Slaves in South Carolina make their way to a nearby church on Sunday.

the Bible stories they knew. Ben fasted regularly on Fridays (as did many Catholics and Methodists at the time) and Harriet often followed his example.

Like her parents, Harriet could not read or write. (Slaves were not allowed to learn to read.) Expected to work from the age of five on, she was never sent to school—and there was no one in her family who could teach her. But there were other opportunities to study biblical traditions: from Anthony Thompson's

THE PARTING "Buy us too."

This historical print shows an enslaved family being torn apart at auction.

son, a physician and minister; from Samuel Green, a black preacher and a friend of the family who lived in the area; and from other preachers who passed through Dorchester County.

Rit, Harriet's mother, tried very hard to keep the family together. Once, when she suspected that Edward Brodess was planning to sell one of her sons to a slave dealer from Georgia, she took her son into the woods and hid him there for over a month. Edward went to her cabin and ordered her to return her son. Rit refused—complying only when Edward assured her he would not sell him.

Anthony Thompson's will stipulated that Ben would become free in 1841. Anthony also promised Ben the use of 10 acres of land during his lifetime and the right to cut and sell the timber on the land to support his family. Anthony died in 1836, and his son Dr. Anthony Thompson manumitted, or freed, Ben five years later. Ben continued to work for Dr. Thompson—but as a free man who would collect a salary.

The number of free blacks in Maryland had increased dramatically, rising from 8,000 in 1790 to almost 53,000 in 1830. One third of the African-Americans living in Maryland were free. They could work for pay and could choose their own home, although there were restrictions on the housing that was made available to them. Other rights were also denied them. Free African-Americans could not vote, bear arms, or testify against whites in court. Many, despite their free status, lived in fear of being kidnapped and sold.

A farmer with little business sense, Edward Brodess felt compelled to sell his slaves to help solve his financial problems. Linah and Soph, Harriet's two sisters, were handcuffed and put in jail. They were then taken south and sold. The separation was cruel—all the more so because they were forced to leave behind Linah's two children. The family, now divided, was heartbroken.

Slaves were often chained one to the other after being captured or sold.

Dr. Anthony Thompson maintained a city residence in Cambridge (shown here) and a country house in Poplar Neck.

In 1844, at the age of 22, Harriet married a free black man named John Tubman. Born in northern Dorchester County, he was 10 years older than Harriet. Three African-American families with the last name of Tubman lived in the area, but the family to which John belonged has not been identified. Also unknown are the details of Harriet and John's first meeting, courtship, or wedding. It is assumed that they lived in the Poplar Neck area, north of Dorchester, on land owned by Dr. Anthony Thompson.

Dr. Thompson took care of his many interests—the practice of medicine, the opening of a drugstore in Cambridge, his appointment as school commissioner there, and his participation in the Sons of Temperance, an organization that campaigned against the use of alcohol. In 1847, Harriet was hired out to Dr. Thompson. Harriet and John wanted to purchase Harriet's freedom, but they did not have the money. It would take many years to earn sufficient funds. Harriet remained the property of Edward Brodess— and prayed every night to be rid of him. She did not want to suffer the same fate as her sisters.

Harriet had long suspected that Atthow Pattison, her mother's first slave master, may very well have provided for Rit's freedom in his will. In the late 1840s she hired a lawyer to check into Mr. Pattison's will. What she found confirmed her suspicions. The will stated that Rit, Mr. Pattison's other female slaves, and their children, would be granted their

Literacy among African-Americans

Enslavers discouraged African-Americans from learning to read and write for fear that the knowledge would give them power. In many Southern states it was illegal to teach a slave to read or write; those who did could be fined, imprisoned, or whipped. Slaves who were caught learning to read or write were often beaten; sometimes their fingers or toes were amputated. Nevertheless, many did learn to read and write and several wrote their own autobiographies.

freedom at the age of 45. When Edward Brodess inherited Rit from his mother, he may never have known the stipulations of his great-grandfather's will—or he may have known and chosen to

> *"Every time I saw a white man I was afraid of being carried away."*
>
> –Harriet to Benjamin Drew

ignore them. In either case, Rit had spent the last decade of her life enslaved when she should have been free. The sale of Harriet's sisters was also a clear violation of the law. (A slave who had received the promise of manumission could not be sold out of state.) Harriet felt angered and betrayed—she could not trust her master. If he was capable of such deception, he could do anything. Her future and that of her family lay in his hands.

Edward Brodess died on March 7, 1849, at the age of 47. His will stated that his wife, Eliza, would receive the use and hire of his slaves while she lived and that after her death his estate would be passed on to his children. Therefore none of his slaves could be sold out of state. But Harriet did not trust Eliza—after all, Edward had sold her two sisters.

Harriet grew restless. Her dreams became more frequent and alarming. In the middle of the night she would wake up haunted by the fear that she would be dragged away. She saw horsemen coming and heard women and children screaming. Her husband, John, tried to calm her. But Harriet would not be reassured.

chapter **5**

North Star

When Edward Brodess died, he left his wife, Eliza, with large debts—more than $1,000. The court required her to pay them, and Eliza obtained a loan from a neighbor to do so. She also made arrangements to sell Kessiah, Harriet's niece. Harriet feared she might be next, and she was determined not to let that happen. Other slaves from the Eastern Shore had escaped—Harriet had heard talk. The woods offered a place to hide and the stars could help show the way. Word had spread that there were people, white and black, who would help. They opened up their homes to fugitives or gave directions, and they provided a warm meal.

After Harriet and her brothers tried to escape, Eliza Brodess posted this advertisement in the *Cambridge Democrat* (using Harriet's nickname, Minty).

THREE HUNDRED DOLLARS REWARD.

RANAWAY from the subscriber on Monday the 17th ult., three negroes, named as follows: HARRY, aged about 19 years, has on one side of his neck a wen, just under the ear, he is of a dark chestnut color, about 5 feet 8 or 9 inches hight; BEN, aged aged about 25 years, is very quick to speak when spoken to, he is of a chestnut color, about six feet high; MINTY, aged about 27 years, is of a chestnut color, fine looking, and about 5 feet high. One hundred dollars reward will be given for each of the above named negroes, if taken out of the State, and $50 each if taken in the State. They must be lodged in Baltimore, Easton or Cambridge Jail, in Maryland.

ELIZA ANN BRODESS,
Near Bucktown, Dorchester county, Md.
Oct. 3d, 1849.

On September 17, 1849, Harriet made a courageous decision. She would leave the Poplar Neck area she had called home for several years. She would head north—risking her life to win her freedom. She would find her way through the Underground

Railroad, the name given to the secret escape routes that the slaves used.

Harriet's husband John stayed behind. But her two brothers Ben and Henry accompanied her. Their journey was a dangerous one. Although they moved cautiously, they might be caught at any moment. Few people could be trusted to come to their aid.

Eliza posted a notice offering a reward—$100 for the return of each of the three slaves if they were captured out of state, and $50 for each if they were found in state. The notice provided not only their names but approximate ages and physical descriptions. The fear of capture became too much for Ben and Henry. They also argued with Harriet about directions. Scared and frustrated, the brothers persuaded Harriet to return to Poplar Neck.

But Harriet did not remain long on Dr. Thompson's property. She would set out again—this time without her brothers.

"Underground Road"

The term "Underground Road" was coined in 1831. When Tice Davids, a fugitive from Kentucky, swam to freedom across the Ohio River, his master pursued him—but found no one who could help him find the runaway slave. The master concluded that the fugitive had used "an underground road." Later the term "Underground Railroad" became popular to describe the secret routes on which fugitives traveled as they sought freedom. Those who escaped were called "passengers." "Conductors" guided them along the way while those who provided shelter were called "station masters."

Fugitives of the *Pearl*

Not all fugitives found freedom. On April 15, 1848, 77 escaped slaves boarded the *Pearl* in Washington, D.C., and set sail along the Potomac River. They were captured two days later, and most were sold. Two sisters, Mary and Emily Edmondson, were eventually freed. Mary became a schoolteacher in Washington. The captain of the *Pearl* was tried in a well-publicized case that aroused antislavery sentiment in the North.

Harriet wanted to prepare her family and friends for her departure, but did not want to be overheard discussing her plans. She sang a song that would be interpreted as a farewell:

"I'll meet you in the morning,
I'm bound for the promised land,
On the other side of Jordan,
Bound for the promised land."

The song had a special meaning for Harriet. In biblical times the Israelites crossed the River Jordan to reach the land God had promised them; there they were rewarded for their struggles. For Harriet, reaching the promised land meant only one thing: freedom from slavery.

For most of the journey she traveled by foot—90 miles (145 km) through swampland. She spent the days hidden in the woods, sleeping on a bed of pine needles or sinking into a cushion of cool moss. She walked at night, silently so as not to arouse suspicion. And, just as many fugitives before her had done, she used the North Star as a guide. This star, one of the brightest and most prominent in the night sky, always appears to the north and can be used for navigation. For Harriet it became a great source both of comfort and of hope. She kept her eye on the star throughout the evening and well past midnight. Then, as the star faded and dawn broke, Harriet would grow tired and be ready to rest.

The North Star maintains its position in the north, as other stars appear to spin around it, as shown in this long-exposure photograph of the night sky.

Harriet had no second thoughts about the choice she had made: "I had reasoned this out in my mind; there was one of two things I had a right to, liberty or death; if I could not have one I would have the other, for no man should take me alive; I should fight for my liberty as long as my strength lasted, and when the time came for me to go, the Lord would let them take me."

On occasion she found refuge in the home of a stranger. A Quaker woman took her in and gave her the names of two people who might help her. Before leaving, Harriet gave her host

"There was one of two things I had a right to, liberty or death; if I could not have one I would have the other."

–Harriet Tubman, as quoted by Sarah Bradford

a quilt to thank her for all she had done. (Several Quaker abolitionists lived close to Dr. Thompson's land, so it is not surprising that Harriet felt comfortable in the company of Quakers and found those she could trust.)

After traveling from Maryland to Delaware, Harriet went on to Philadelphia—a city that was home to 20,000

African-Americans, almost all of them free, and many of them fugitives who were starting a new life. Here former slaves

Harriet and other fugitives often used disguises as they traveled north. Here Harriet is dressed as a man and is accompanied by another African-American.

found jobs and established their own homes. They went to church and shopped in the market. No one would stop them— they could come and go as they pleased.

"I was a stranger in a strange land," Harriet said after arriving in Philadelphia in 1849.

Harriet's newfound liberty in Philadelphia was a great cause for rejoicing. "When I found I had crossed that line, I looked at my hands to see if I was the same person. There was such a glory over every thing; the sun came like gold through the trees, and over the fields, and I felt like I was in heaven," she said. But the moment was bittersweet. Harriet later said she was "a stranger in a strange land." There was no one to welcome her to the land of freedom.

The Pennsylvania Society for the Abolition of Slavery

The Pennsylvania Society for the Abolition of Slavery grew out of the Society for the Relief of Free Negroes Unlawfully Held in Bondage (the first antislavery society). Members of this organization helped fugitives and promoted the abolition of slavery through petitions and public speeches. From 1845 to 1850, the well-known African-American abolitionist Robert Purvis served as president of the organization.

She had left behind not only her husband, but her parents, her brothers, her sisters, and her friends. It hurt to be without them. It hurt too to know that many of them were still enslaved.

Harriet soon met people—both black and white—who befriended her. They were active in the abolitionist movement, and some were members of the Pennsylvania Society for the Abolition of Slavery. They helped former slaves make new homes in Philadelphia or assisted those who wanted to journey farther north. They were yet another part of the Underground Railroad.

Eager for her family to enjoy the same freedom she did, Harriet resolved to make that possible. "I would make a home for them in the North, and the Lord helping me, I would bring them all here." But first she would have to earn enough money to pay for travel and food.

Harriet found short-term employment in Philadelphia. She took on a variety of jobs as a household servant and cook.

The Mount Vernon Hotel was one of Cape May's many resorts. Built in 1852, it could accommodate more than 2,000 guests.

During the summer months she traveled to Cape May, a delightful resort town at the tip of the New Jersey shore, 90 miles (145 km) from Philadelphia. There she worked as a cook and laundress.

Harriet had started as a passenger on the Underground Railroad. It would not be long before she would take on a different role and become one of its most famous conductors. She believed that God had spoken to her—it was her responsibility to answer his call. "He gave me strength," she said, "and he set the North Star in the heavens; he meant I should be free."

6

The Underground Railroad

In December 1850, word reached Philadelphia that Eliza Brodess would try again to sell Harriet's niece Kessiah and Kessiah's two children. (Her earlier attempt had failed.) Harriet felt compelled to act. She traveled south to Maryland for the first time since she had left home. She met Kessiah's husband John Bowley, a free man, in Baltimore, and the two came up with a clever scheme.

On the day of the auction, Kessiah and her children were taken to the steps of the courthouse in Cambridge, Maryland. The bidding began as scheduled. Once the price was agreed upon, the auctioneer took a break. As soon as he returned he asked the buyer to come forward with the payment—but the buyer was nowhere to be found. His identity remained a mystery.

Only later did it become clear that John Bowley was the highest bidder. During the commotion that followed

Eliza Brodess placed this advertisement to sell Kessiah in the *Cambridge Democrat* in August 1849. The sale did not go through and Eliza tried again the next year.

NEGRO FOR SALE.

I WILL sell at public sale to the highest bidder for cash, at the Court house door in the town of Cambridge, on MONDAY the 10th day of September next, a negro woman named KIZZIAH, aged about 25 years. She will be sold for life, and a good title will be given. Attendance given by

JOHN MILLS,
Agent for Elizabeth Brodess.

August 29th 1849.   2w

the bidding, John Bowley had slipped away with Kessiah and the children to a secret location only a few blocks from the courthouse.

While traveling along the Underground Railroad, fugitives hid in unexpected places, such as this opening in the back porch of a house in Cincinnati, Ohio.

Late that evening the fugitives secretly boarded a small boat and set sail on the Chesapeake Bay—taking shelter the next morning in Bodkin's Creek on the Eastern Shore. That night they sailed on to Baltimore. Harriet met them and found a hiding place for them. She let them rest and then took them all the way to Philadelphia.

> *"She will be sold for life, and a good title will be given."*
>
> –from Eliza Brodess's ad announcing the sale of Kessiah

Harriet's next mission was to meet her husband, John, and bring him back with her. In the fall of 1851, she traveled south past Baltimore—returning to Dorchester County. She brought with her a new suit of clothes to give to her husband. But, when she arrived on the Eastern Shore, she discovered that John now had a new wife—a free woman. John wanted to stay where he was and no longer wished to be with Harriet. He did not even want to see her.

At first grieving and angry, Harriet wanted to see John even at the risk of being caught by her old master. She was eager for John to know how upset and hurt she was, so she determined to "make all the trouble she could." Later she thought better of it and saw "how foolish it was just for temper to make mischief." She would show John that if he could do without her, she could do without him.

Since John would not accompany her, Harriet resolved to help others. She would not waste this opportunity. It was difficult to put aside her own sorrow, but she believed the Lord was calling her to help those in need. She took with her four or five fugitives and returned later that year to rescue a larger group, possibly as many as 11. She brought them all safely to Philadelphia.

Harriet's physical stamina helped make her rescue missions possible. She could go for days with little sleep or food. Equally important were her courage and her cunning. Harriet took risks that other people would not take. Although she often put herself in dangerous situations, she did not act foolishly: When she led an expedition, she almost always traveled at night. She might vary her appearance and often provided disguises for the fugitives. Emma Telford, who interviewed Harriet, wrote, "Several times she was at the point of being taken but always escaped by her quick wit or as she calls it 'warnings from Heaven.'"

This cabin belonged to a free African-American in Maryland. In the mid-19th century, there were about 4,000 free African-Americans in Dorchester County, many of whom helped fugitive slaves.

Uncle Tom's Cabin

Uncle Tom's Cabin, an antislavery novel written by Harriet Beecher Stowe (1811–1896), was published in 1852 and would sell more than 300,000 copies in its first year. This book would change the course of history by describing the horrors of enslavement to a national audience. It had first appeared in installments in the *National Era,* a Washington, D.C., abolitionist newspaper.

Singing was something Harriet enjoyed, but it was also a method of distraction. She had such a good voice that most people stopped to listen and forgot any cause for alarm. Harriet would also use the words of her songs to relay secret messages.

She could be heard singing:

"Oh go down, Moses,
Way down into Egypt's land,
Tell old Pharaoh,
Let my people go."

People who understood the code knew these words were a beckoning call to those who wanted to join her.

Ednah Cheney, author of a biographical article published in 1865 in the antislavery journal

Generous and resourceful, the Quaker abolitionist Thomas Garrett was one of the most well-known station masters on the Underground Railroad.

Freedmen's Record, wrote that Harriet would become known by the name of "Moses" —a well-earned title given that she was "the deliverer of her people." She would risk capture—and even death—not only for her family and loved ones, but for strangers as well.

Along the way Harriet met many men and women who became her friends and assisted her in her rescue work. Sam Green, the free African-American preacher from Dorchester County, often hosted Harriet and her "passengers." He would later be sentenced to 10 years in prison for the possession of *Uncle Tom's Cabin*—a novel that was thought to fuel antislavery sentiment.

Thomas Garrett, a Quaker from Wilmington, Delaware, and the owner of a shoe business, often devised methods for the fugitives to cross the Delaware River bridge into Wilmington.

Disembarking from a boat, fugitives prepare to travel by wagon to a safe refuge.

There, he provided the fugitives with nourishment, a place to rest, and a new pair of shoes, if needed. He also gave them courage to continue their journey. He directed them to other safe houses, including the home of William Still, a prominent African-American antislavery activist.

"The idea of being captured by slave hunters or slaveholders seemed never to enter her mind," William Still later wrote. "Her success

William Still recorded testimony from hundreds of fugitives, and compiled their stories into a book published in 1872.

in going into Maryland as she did was attributable to her adventurous spirit and utter disregard of consequences."

Harriet also befriended Lucretia and James Mott, outspoken Quakers who were active in the abolitionist movement. When others dared not reach out to lend Harriet a helping hand, Lucretia came to her aid. Working together, Lucretia and Harriet organized fairs and picnics in Philadelphia to promote the abolitionist cause. And they both became frequent lecturers at antislavery conventions.

Harriet still lapsed into sleep at unexpected moments— sometimes in the midst of conversation. (She may also have been suffering from seizures, the result of the blow to her head she had received as a young girl.) When she awoke she

Lucretia Mott
(1793–1880)

A courageous Quaker, Lucretia Mott was born on Nantucket, off the coast of Cape Cod, and moved to Philadelphia where she became a leader in the peace movement. She also supported the rights of women and African-Americans. She was called "the guiding spirit" behind the first women's rights convention at Seneca Falls in 1848.

often reported that she had heard voices summoning her to return to Maryland and bring her people out.

While traveling, Harriet expected her companions to show no signs of weakness. They were not to cry out or complain. She did not hesitate to put a gun to their heads if they considered turning back—or so it was said. Her words, "A live runaway could do great harm by going back, but a dead one could tell no secrets," would become legendary. However, when asked if she ever had to use a gun, she answered that she had not. One way or another she gave those in her care the will to continue on.

In December 1854, Harriet had a premonition that great danger would face her three brothers if she did not save them. She was sure Eliza Brodess would try to sell

PREMONITION

A premonition is a feeling or forewarning of an event that will happen in the future.

them over the Christmas holiday. Desperate to communicate with them, she dictated a letter to Jacob Jackson, a free man who lived near her family. She wrote first of things of little consequence and then ended with a secret message: "Read my letter to the old folks, and give my love to them, and tell my brothers to be always watching unto prayer, and when the good old ship of Zion comes along, to be ready to step aboard." The letter bore not Harriet's signature but that of "William Henry Jackson," the name of Jacob's son.

Harriet and many of the fugitives she helped rescue were beaten and permanently scarred with whips like this one.

Jacob was often suspected of helping fugitive slaves and therefore not allowed to receive a letter unless it had been vetted by a postal inspector. Harriet's letter was opened and read by the inspector. No hidden meaning was discovered so Jacob was allowed to read the letter. After finishing the letter Jacob declared, "That letter can't be meant for me. . . . I can't make head nor tail of it." He walked off, leaving the letter behind. But as soon as he left he sent word to Harriet's brothers that their sister was on her way.

Harriet arrived in Dorchester County the day before Christmas and learned that her three brothers—Robert, Henry, and Ben—were to be auctioned on December 26.

Ben and Henry met her and accompanied her to Poplar Neck where their parents lived. Ben told Harriet that he wanted his fiancée, Jane Kane, to join them. Jane's master,

> "A live runaway could do great harm by going back, but a dead one could tell no secrets."
>
> –attributed to Harriet Tubman

Horatio Jones, was one of the more cruel enslavers on the Eastern Shore. He flogged his slaves with no provocation, gave them little or no food, and made them suffer in the cold. He had also forbidden Ben and Jane to marry.

Ben bought a new suit of men's clothes for Jane to wear as a disguise. Without letting anyone notice, he threw the

This 1850 engraving shows the flight of a group of Maryland fugitives on their way to a Delaware station on the Underground Railroad.

Before escaping to Canada, Harriet's brothers hid in a corn crib near their parents' cabin.

bundle over the Joneses' garden fence. Jane knew where to look—she found the clothes, put them on, and wandered past the Joneses' house and out the gate. No one was the least suspicious. Before long, Jane met her fiancé in Poplar Neck.

Years later Harriet would describe the difficult choice her brother Robert had to make. He wanted neither to be sold nor to leave behind his two children and his wife, pregnant with their third. He came close to walking out the door, but then his wife went into labor. Robert stayed with her until their baby, a girl they named Harriet, was born. After the birth, Robert thought he had best slip away—he did, yet he could hear his wife's sobs through the open window. He went back inside, but then his wife urged him to go. She would rather have him flee to the North than be sold into the South.

Robert traveled the 40 miles (64 km) to Poplar Neck to meet Harriet and his brothers—all hidden in the corn crib near his parents' cabin. They did not want their mother to know they planned

CORN CRIB

Farmers store their corn in a hut or small barn called a corn crib.

to escape for fear she would become too upset. However, they did send word to their father. He brought them food but was careful not to look at them or stay to visit. Once his sons' absence was noticed, he would be questioned, and he wanted to answer convincingly that he had seen none of his children over the holidays.

On Christmas Day, Harriet, her brothers, and Jane walked over to the cabin and looked at Rit through the window. She was expecting her sons to join her for Christmas dinner. Seated in her rocking chair, she waited. But no one entered the cabin—no one knocked on the door. Her children took great pains not to be seen by her although it made them very sad. Just as they were ready to depart, their father, Ben, came outside to join them. Tying his handkerchief over his eyes, he walked with them a short distance. He could still say he had not seen his sons.

Levi Coffin and his wife, Catherine, pictured here in a painting by Charles T. Webber, assisted thousands of fugitives. Levi Coffin was known as the President of the Underground Railroad.

This New England home was a station on the Underground Railroad. Fugitives may have slept in the attic, the cellar, or a hidden room.

Once Eliza Brodess realized the brothers had disappeared, she sent slave catchers to find them. When they questioned Ben and Rit, both parents said they had not seen their sons. Rit said she had waited for her sons all Christmas Day—but they never appeared. The slave catchers moved on and found no traces of the fugitives.

Harriet brought her brothers and Jane safely out of Maryland and took them to Thomas Garrett's home in Wilmington. In a letter dated December 29, 1854, Thomas writes of sending Harriet, six men, and one woman to Allen Agnew's—no doubt a station on the Underground Railroad. He also gave the group two dollars for new shoes and money for a carriage. The party made their way to William Still's antislavery office in Philadelphia.

There the runaways would choose new names to help conceal their identities. The Ross brothers took a new last name—they chose "Stewart," the name of a prominent white family on the Eastern Shore. Ben became "James," Robert became "John," Henry became "William Henry," and Jane became "Catherine." William Still kept a record of the name changes as well as each fugitive's description, age, and family members.

But the party did not stop in Philadelphia. They would not be safe there and would have to go much further—all the way to Canada: U.S. laws had changed, and it was becoming increasingly dangerous for fugitives to live peacefully even in the Northern states. After the passage of the Fugitive Slave Act in 1850, Harriet said, "I wouldn't trust Uncle Sam with my people any longer, so I brought them all clear to Canada."

The new law required that runaway slaves be returned to their masters even if they were caught outside of the state from which they had escaped. A $1,000 fine was to be imposed on any officer who did not enforce the law. Slave catchers were seen on the streets of Philadelphia just as they were in New York and Boston—a reminder to many that fugitives still faced great risks, and that the United States no longer offered a safe home for those who had been enslaved.

Dating from the 1850s, this is the earliest known picture of Harriet Tubman.

chapter 7

The Promised Land

Former slaves who had fled to the North faced many obstacles—a colder climate, little or no money, unemployment. In the beginning they often had to depend on the kindness of strangers for food and shelter. Their greatest fear was capture. Slave catchers carried guns, brought with them fierce dogs, and were fueled by the promise of rewards, sometimes as much as $4,000. Canada, on the other hand, offered not only

Fugitives hid wherever they could to avoid capture. This photograph shows a cave that offered welcome shelter.

This drawing from the antislavery newspaper *Emancipator* illustrates the cruelty of the slave catchers.

freedom—but also safety from those who would take it away.

In 1793, British Canada's Lieutenant Governor John Graves Simcoe introduced and helped pass an act "to prevent the further introduction of Slaves, and to limit the terms of contracts for servitude within the Province." By 1833, slavery was abolished in most of the British Empire. The number of African-Americans who came to Canada would multiply—before the Civil War, this British province would become home to as many as 60,000 African-Americans.

Newly arrived refugees in Canada often became farmers, cooks, builders, and painters. They sent their children to school and organized their own churches. They found land cheap enough to buy, and those who owned property were allowed to vote. Not only fugitives but missionaries, black and white, traveled to what they called "the promised land," where it was possible to start a new life.

William Still had given Harriet, her brothers, and Catherine (as Ben's fiancée was now called) money to travel by train to

MISSIONARY

A missionary undertakes to establish a religious organization and often aids those in need.

Albany, the capital of New York, and then on to Buffalo. They did little to attract attention and most passengers ignored them. However, whenever someone approached Harriet she pretended to read a book or newspaper so as not to arouse suspicion.

In January 1855, Harriet led her family across the suspension bridge over the Niagara River into Canada— and to freedom. They made a home in a town called St. Catharines, only 11 miles (18 km) from the border.

When Harriet first visited St. Catharines a few years earlier, 300 of its 2,500 residents were black. In 10 years the black population would almost double—many would come from the Eastern Shore of Maryland. The sawmills and the Welland Canal Company

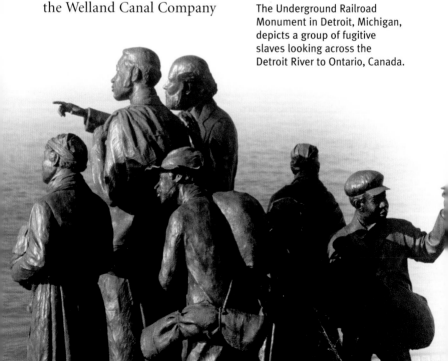

The Underground Railroad Monument in Detroit, Michigan, depicts a group of fugitive slaves looking across the Detroit River to Ontario, Canada.

For many refugee slaves, reaching Niagara Falls meant achieving freedom.

employed a large number of workers. Newcomers also found jobs in the hotels and spas built around the area's mineral springs.

Here in St. Catharines, African-Americans enjoyed much greater freedom than they had in the United States. Yet they were still denied rights and privileges that the white population took for granted. They could work at the hotels but were not welcome guests. The climate in St. Catharines was also harsher than it was in Maryland. Not only was the temperature much colder, but the nights were longer. With no warm clothes and no heat, Harriet's family did not fare well. Still, they survived the winter and Harriet would continue to bring fugitives to St. Catharines.

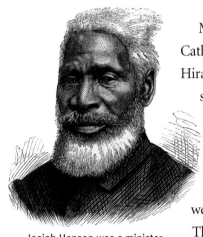

Josiah Henson was a minister who helped free many slaves, and was a model for Uncle Tom in Harriet Beecher Stowe's book.

Many of the new arrivals in St. Catharines were met by Reverend Hiram Wilson, a missionary who had studied at Oberlin Theological Seminary. Together with Reverend Josiah Henson, a former slave, he had founded a settlement for refugees in western Ontario, called "Dawn." This organization provided education and job training. In 1849, Reverend Wilson moved to St. Catharines where he founded a second settlement for fugitives and helped build several schools. Reverend Wilson was a great admirer of Harriet Tubman and he assisted her in caring for the fugitives she led to St. Catharines.

A few years later Reverend Wilson was criticized for financial mismanagement and had to disband his activities. Harriet and her brother William Henry then organized the Fugitive Aid Society of St. Catharines to take on much of the same work. Several fugitives who had escaped from

Harriet was determined to make a better life in St. Catharines for those she had helped rescue.

"Moses has got the charm."

–a refugee, about Harriet Tubman

Dorchester County became leaders in the society. They collected and distributed clothing and raised funds to aid the refugees.

In all, Harriet made a total of 10 to 13 rescue missions. It was not only her bravery and cunning that made her expeditions a success. She also connected with people along the way and developed strong relationships. Her friends on the Underground Railroad had no trouble recognizing her—she was petite, dressed simply, and almost always wore black. A long full black skirt and a black hat were her trademarks. People who met her were entertained by her wit, and those who heard her sing were impressed.

Many of the Canadian refugees believed God had given Harriet a special power. They would

A group of former slaves who had settled in Ontario, Canada, before the Civil War, posed for this picture in 1892.

William Wells Brown (c. 1814–1884)

Born a slave in Lexington, Kentucky, and raised in St. Louis, Missouri, William Wells Brown worked on a steamboat before escaping to Cleveland, Ohio. There, he worked as a waiter and steamboat operator—often ferrying fugitives across Lake Erie to freedom. He later became a leader in the antislavery movement, and was also a playwright, novelist, and lecturer who traveled throughout the United States, Canada, and Europe.

say, "Moses has got the charm." William Wells Brown, who was born into slavery and escaped to become a conductor on the Underground Railroad and a well-known author, explained it this way: "Yes, and the woman herself felt that she had the charm, and this feeling, no doubt, nerved her up, gave her courage, and made all who followed her feel safe in her hands."

Just as Harriet had taken jobs in Philadelphia and Cape May to help fund her rescue missions, she also found work in Canada to supplement her trips south. She chopped wood not only to buy food for her family, but also to pay travel expenses—including train tickets for some of her Underground Railroad "passengers."

On one journey Harriet guided a woman accompanied by two small children and a baby. Harriet kept the baby in a basket wrapped in a comforter, and sometimes during the day had to give the baby laudanum,

> *"No fugitive was ever captured who had Moses for a leader."*
>
> –William Wells Brown

a medication then used as a pain reliever, to quiet him. Fortunately, this stopped the baby from crying and ensured a safe journey. Some of her Canadian friends, fearing she might not always have such good fortune, would say, "Harriet Tubman will go once too often and she won't return." They were wrong. Harriet always came back and, as William Wells Brown said, "No fugitive was ever captured who had Moses for a leader."

One of Harriet's most difficult missions took place in April 1857. A month before, a group of eight fugitives had escaped from Dorchester County to Dover, Delaware, where they were caught and arrested. They then broke out of the jail, ran away, and disbanded. The fugitives spent a night in Ben and Rit's cabin before heading north and, within a couple of months, they had all reached Canada.

In St. Catharines, Harriet worshipped at the British Methodist Episcopal Church, built by African-Americans and completed in 1855. She rented a small house across the street from the church.

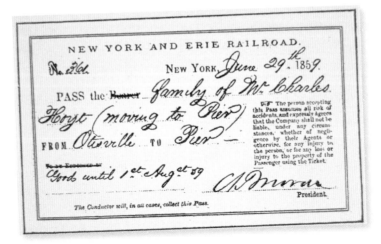

NEW YORK AND ERIE RAILROAD.

No. 261. NEW YORK, *June 29th 1859.*

PASS the ~~Bearer~~ *Family of Mr Charles.*

Hoyt (moving to Pier)

FROM *Otisville* TO *Pier* —

~~~~ *Goods until 1st August 59* President.

The Conductor will, in all cases, collect this Pass.

> The person accepting this Pass assumes all risk of accidents and expressly agrees that the Company shall be liable, under any circumstances, whether of negligence by their Agents or otherwise, for any injury to the person, or for any loss or injury to the property of the Passenger using the Ticket.

This well-publicized escape attracted the attention—and anger— of slaveholders in Maryland. Dr. Anthony Thompson knew Ben had been involved, and advised him to leave the area. Even though Ben was technically free, there was a good chance he would be arrested for aiding the "Dover Eight" in their escape. Harriet received word that her parents were in danger and immediately headed for the Eastern Shore to bring them north to Canada.

Harriet helped pay for train passes like this one to help those fleeing to Canada.

Anthony Thompson's will had set in motion Ben's manumission. On June 11, 1855, Ben paid Eliza Brodess $20 to purchase his wife's freedom, too. But both Ben and Rit feared they would no longer be able to enjoy the freedom to which they were legally entitled. Ben's recent actions had alarmed the authorities, and he now ran a high risk of being captured.

Harriet procured an old horse with a collar made of straw and a makeshift wagon. She seated her parents on the wagon and drove the rickety contraption all the way to Wilmington. There Thomas Garrett gave her $30 to help cover the cost of train tickets. He also arranged to sell the horse and send Harriet the proceeds. Harriet and her parents stopped in Philadelphia, where they met William Still, and then traveled on to Rochester, New York. Maria Porter, the secretary of the Rochester Ladies' Anti-Slavery Society, took them in. After two weeks, they crossed into Canada.

Although the surroundings were different from the home they had known, Ben and Rit were now among loved ones. They soon settled in and enjoyed the company of their sons— and the grandchildren they had never met. Ben and Rit were now close to 70 years old—few people that age had made such a long journey to the promised land.

Anthony Burns and the Fugitive Slave Act

In 1854, Anthony Burns escaped from slavery in Virginia and fled to Boston, where he was arrested. A rescue attempt led to a riot and the death of a U.S. marshal. Burns was tried and sent back to his master. This case served to fuel anger against the passage of the Fugitive Slave Act, the 1850 law that allowed for the return of escaped slaves.

chapter **8**

"Moses" in Auburn

"I have seen hundreds of escaped slaves, but I never saw one who was willing to go back and be a slave. . . . I think slavery is the next thing to hell. If a person would send another into bondage, he would, it appears to me, be bad enough to send him into hell."

Harriet spoke these words to Benjamin Drew, an abolitionist author who recorded testimony from fugitive slaves in Canada. Her reputation was becoming widespread: Harriet risked her life to free loved ones, friends, and those in need— she believed fervently in the antislavery cause and she did not hesitate to let her voice be heard. She would meet and join forces with all the well-known abolitionists of her time.

In 1856, John Brown, a bold and determined abolitionist, had led an insurrection against the proslavery forces active in the Kansas Territory, where his sons lived. Not content to stop there, he resolved to lead an armed slave rebellion in Virginia.

Traveling throughout Canada, writer Benjamin Drew published testimonies from hundreds of former slaves, helping draw attention to the brutality of slavery.

In April 1858, Harriet's friend
Reverend Jermain Loguen, a bishop
in the African Methodist Episcopal
Church in Syracuse, New York,

Harriet befriended many of the antislavery activists pictured here in a painting by Jerry Pinkney, including Jermain Loguen, Lucretia Mott, Frederick Douglass, and William Still.

arranged for John Brown to meet Harriet. He took an instant
liking to her. Impressed with tales of her rescue missions, he
called her "General Tubman" and asked her to join his cause.

Shortly before this first encounter, Harriet had been
both haunted and puzzled by a vivid dream: Wandering

through a wilderness filled with rocks and bushes, she had seen the head of a serpent appear between the rocks and transform into a man with a flowing beard. Two other heads rose up—and then a large crowd of people struck down the heads. Now Harriet saw a connection between the dream and Brown, and she would attach great significance to it.

John Brown, like Harriet, felt called to put an end to slavery.

As Harriet thought about her dream, her faith in this rebel's ability to lead increased. She wanted African-Americans to hear John Brown speak and agreed to gather a group of fugitives in the home she rented for her family. Brown's fiery language and passion energized them. But the Virginia rebellion he was planning would not take place as scheduled—Brown could not raise sufficient funds.

In the summer of 1858, Harriet traveled to New England to promote her cause. John Brown introduced her to the abolitionist newspaper editor William Lloyd Garrison and his wife with these words of praise: "I bring you one of the best and

> *"I was beaten . . . until the blood ran from my mouth and nose."*
>
> –Catherine Stewart (Harriet's sister-in-law) to Benjamin Drew

bravest persons in the continent." Harriet also became acquainted with Franklin B. Sanborn, a

> **TRANSCENDENTALIST**
>
> A Transcendentalist believes that the divine—or spiritual—state is the most important guiding principle.

schoolteacher and writer, who supported John Brown. She made frequent trips to Concord, Massachusetts, where she was a guest of two transcendentalist writers, Ralph Waldo Emerson and Bronson Alcott (father of the children's book author Louisa May Alcott). Mary Peabody Mann, an educator and writer, became another close friend.

At first Harriet spoke to small gatherings in people's homes, but gradually her audiences grew larger. On July 4, 1859, she spoke at a Massachusetts Anti-Slavery Society meeting in Framingham, Massachusetts. Introduced to her audience as "Moses," she shared her own experiences as a former slave—and as a conductor on the Underground Railroad. "She has great dramatic power; the scene rises before you as she saw it, and her voice and language change with her different actors," Ednah Cheney reported.

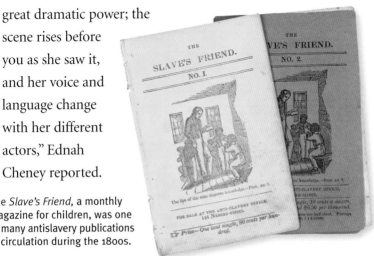

The *Slave's Friend*, a monthly magazine for children, was one of many antislavery publications in circulation during the 1800s.

The *Liberator*

In 1831, William Lloyd Garrison published the first issue of the *Liberator*. This antislavery newspaper was published weekly until the end of the Civil War in 1865. James Forten, a successful African-American businessman, provided financial support and also contributed articles. A fervent abolitionist, Garrison believed in the "immediate and complete" emancipation of all slaves. He advocated "passive resistance"—the use of nonviolent means to end slavery and achieve social reforms.

Speaking frequently throughout the summer, Harriet shared stories of the cruel oppression she had suffered while enslaved.Wherever she went, she drew large crowds and gained support for the abolitionist movement. She had never learned to read—some historians have speculated that the blow to the head she suffered as a young girl caused a lasting learning disability. Still, she was a magnificent storyteller. Listening to every word, the audience was enthralled. They were moved by her story, charmed by her manner, and won over by her cause.

Frederick Douglass welcomed Harriet into his home in Rochester, New York. This famous abolitionist sheltered a large number of fugitives as they passed through New York on their way to Canada, and many of them were fugitives Harriet brought with her on her way to Canada. Like Harriet, he too had been a former slave and was born on the Eastern

Shore. Their families may have known each other; in any case they shared many ties to the community. Douglass, a well-established public figure, became a long-time admirer of Harriet's devotion to freedom and her willingness to take risks.

Harriet traveled over hills and through forests, past beautiful blue lakes to Auburn, a town in the Finger Lakes region of New York, 55 miles (89 km) from Rochester. She was introduced to Lucretia Mott's sister Martha Coffin Wright and her husband, David Wright, an attorney. Martha shared her sister's abolitionist sentiments, and also sheltered

Frederick Douglass (c. 1818–1895)

Frederick Douglass was born into slavery in Talbot County, Maryland. His mistress, Sophia Auld, taught him to read—and broke the law in doing so. In 1838, disguised as a sailor, Douglass escaped and traveled by train to Philadelphia and then to New York. Seven years later, he wrote *Narrative of the Life of Frederick Douglass, an American Slave*. He traveled throughout Great Britain giving antislavery lectures.

After British supporters purchased his freedom, he returned to the United States and settled in Buffalo, New York. He became a great orator and the publisher of the *North Star*, an abolitionist newspaper. After the Civil War, Douglass held several official government positions. In 1877, he moved to Cedar Hill, overlooking the Anacostia River in Washington, D.C. His house still stands at the site today.

fugitives in her home. She would be a good friend to Harriet throughout her life.

David Wright's law partner, William H. Seward, and his wife, Frances, would also become Harriet's loyal supporters. William Seward, at the time a U.S. senator, offered to sell Harriet a parcel of land—with a wood-frame house and a barn. He had inherited the property, on the outskirts of the town of Auburn, from his father-in-law. His price was reasonable: $1,200. He would require a $25 down payment; no date was set for the payment of the remainder of the money. Senator Seward had sold inexpensive houses to other people in need; still it was unusual in the United States to sell land to an African-American woman—and a fugitive slave, at that.

Harriet worried about her parents. The winter in St. Catharines had been difficult for them. The climate was too harsh— Ben and Rit did not like

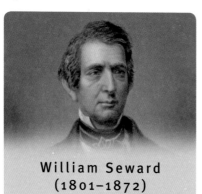

William Seward
(1801–1872)

William Seward practiced law with his father-in-law, Judge Elijah Miller, before entering politics. He would serve as New York governor, U.S. senator, and secretary of state. William and his wife, Frances, became abolitionists after visiting the South in 1835. They would not forget seeing child slaves, tied together, forced to walk on the road as they left their families behind. The Sewards would later hide fugitive slaves in their home in Auburn.

the snow and ice and they did not take well to the change. Eventually, Harriet decided to move her family to Auburn. The town may not have offered a dramatic difference in temperature, but Harriet, her parents, and two of her brothers—John and William Henry—would find a friendly community where other African-Americans had made their home.

William Henry Stewart moved from St. Catharines to join his sister Harriet in Auburn.

Not everyone in Auburn shared the Wrights' and the Sewards' abolitionist views, but those who did made Harriet feel welcome. The family made the move to their new house on South Street, and enjoyed the new surroundings, the farmland, and the apple orchard. John and William Henry had children to support, so it fell to Harriet to raise money to care for her parents.

By the fall of 1859, John Brown was prepared to stage his rebellion in the South. He had accumulated what he thought would be sufficient funds and had collected 200 guns as well as ammunition. But Frederick Douglass was skeptical and no longer supported him. And Harriet became ill and could not offer the assistance she had planned to provide.

On Sunday, October 16, Brown and 19 followers attacked the armory at Harpers Ferry in what is now West Virginia,

An on-the-scene reporter and artist drew this sketch of the Harpers Ferry raid as the U.S. marines stormed the armory.

planning to take over and raid the facility and distribute the weapons to slaves so they might free themselves. By Tuesday, U.S. marines led by Colonel Robert E. Lee had seized the armory. In the gun battle that followed, 10 of the raiders were killed—including two of John Brown's sons. John Brown was captured, tried, and found guilty. He was sentenced to be hanged.

The execution would take place on December 2, 1859. Harriet was undone. Her dream became clear: The fallen heads were those of John Brown and his two sons. Harriet foresaw that the impact of the rebellion would have far-reaching consequences: John Brown's death would only incite abolitionist fever. In a letter dictated to her friend Martha Wright, Harriet said, "He did more in dying than 100 men would have, in living."

> *"He did more in dying than 100 men would have, in living."*
>
> —Harriet Tubman, speaking of John Brown

Eager to keep Brown's cause alive, Harriet traveled to Boston to speak at the New England Anti-Slavery Conference. On the way, she stopped in Troy, New York. Harriet learned that a fugitive slave named Charles Nalle, the father of six children, had been arrested there, and was to be sent back to Culpeper, Virginia.

Knowing the danger Charles faced if he were sent back, Harriet went to the office in Troy where he was being detained. On the way she encouraged antislavery activists to gather outside the building. Moving slowly and bending forward to appear weak and frail, she instructed a group of young boys to yell "fire." Chaos ensued. People shouted and ran in various directions. A U.S. marshal tied Charles's hands together and pushed him through the crowd to a wagon that waited outside.

The Last Moments of John Brown, by Thomas Hovenden, shows Brown hugging an African-American child as he is led to his execution.

Abolitionists traveled to Boston to attend meetings of the New England Anti-Slavery Conference.

Harriet sprang into action. No longer pretending to be a feeble old lady, she knocked the officer aside and grabbed Charles. She pulled and dragged him toward the river. Every time an officer tried to stop her, she fought back—but never let go of Charles. She threw him over her shoulder like a sack of flour. Several policemen beat her over the head with a club, but still she kept going and shouted out her favorite saying, "Give me liberty or give me death!" By the time she reached the river, her clothes were torn and she had lost her shoes. But Charles was safe. A boatman was ready to take him across the river. Harriet's rescue attempt was successful—her physical strength (and a little cunning) had made it possible.

This episode did not stop Harriet from attending the conference in Boston and giving a passionate antislavery speech. Once again, she was introduced as "Moses." William Lloyd Garrison's newspaper, the *Liberator,* reported on her address: "She told the story of her adventures in a modest but quaint and amusing style."

In 1862, Harriet made another trip to Maryland. This time she brought back a 10-year old niece named Margaret Stewart. Frances Seward—and Frances's sister Lazette

Worden, a widow active in the abolitionist and women's rights movement—would both care for the child and make Margaret feel at home in a nursery filled with toys and books. It is unclear why Harriet brought Margaret to Auburn, since Margaret's mother was a free woman and the young girl came from a comfortable background. (Margaret remembers that her family owned a pair of chestnut horses and a carriage.) Much speculation surrounds this mysterious rescue. Perhaps Harriet kidnapped Margaret, taking her without her mother's permission. It has been suggested that Margaret reminded Harriet of the daughter she never had. Another theory, albeit one that is unsubstantiated, is that Harriet may have given birth to Margaret before she escaped from Maryland and left her to be raised by her brother's family. In any case, Harriet would always remain close to Margaret; indeed the young girl closely resembled Harriet and always received special attention.

Harriet may very well have favored Margaret, but she would not stay tied to Auburn to care for her. Before long she would answer another call.

Margaret Stewart, Harriet's niece, played with the toys she found in the Sewards' nursery.

chapter **9**

"Forever Free of Servitude"

O n December 20, 1860, the citizens of South Carolina voted to secede from the Union. They wanted no part of a government

SECEDE
To secede means to formally withdraw from an organization or political body.

headed by Abraham Lincoln, the newly elected president, who opposed the expansion of slavery. Six states followed suit—Mississippi, Florida, Alabama, Georgia, Louisiana, and Texas—and together they formed the Confederate States of America, or the Confederacy. On April 12, 1861, shots were fired over Fort Sumter, South Carolina. The Civil War had begun. President Lincoln, together with his trusted secretary of state William Seward (Lincoln's former rival in the campaign for the Republican nomination), would lead the United States and its Union army through four years of war. Six hundred thousand Americans would die before the war's end.

Harriet had foreseen the emancipation of her people in a dream she had while visiting the Reverend Henry Highland Garnet, a former slave and well-known

President Abraham Lincoln benefited from discussing issues with Secretary of State William Seward.

orator, at his home in New York. When she came down to breakfast she sang, "My people are free!" Reverend Garnet told her that his grandchildren might see the day of emancipation, but that it would not happen in his lifetime. Harriet remained confident: "I tell you, sir, you'll see it, and you'll see it soon."

Well aware of Harriet's reputation as a leader, her daring, and her quick wit, Governor John Andrew of Massachusetts asked her to serve as a scout and nurse for the Union cause. She accepted the governor's offer and was sent to Beaufort, in the Sea Islands

This woodcut portrait of Harriet during the Civil War was first published in *Scenes in the Life of Harriet Tubman,* by Sarah Bradford.

of South Carolina, an area occupied by Union forces. Harriet quickly made herself useful, distributing clothing, food, and books to the Union soldiers through the YMCA.

YMCA

The Young Men's Christian Association (YMCA) was founded in London by George Williams. The organization sought to provide housing and improve living conditions for men who came to the city to find jobs. In 1851, YMCAs opened in Montreal and Boston. Two years later, Anthony Bowen, a freed slave, founded the first YMCA in Washington, D.C. During the Civil War, YMCAs provided aid to troops and prisoners of war. From the beginning, the association included members of different races, religions, and nationalities.

Lack of sanitation had caused widespread disease. Soldiers were exposed to smallpox, measles, malaria, yellow fever, scarlet fever, and typhoid, and many developed dysentery. Before long, Harriet was serving as a nurse. She learned how to use roots and herbs to treat her patients, and developed an herbal cure for dysentery. It was so successful that doctors insisted she use it to treat all the soldiers in the camp.

Harriet encouraged the newly freed slaves in the Sea Islands to earn money by taking on jobs for the soldiers. They did the washing and sewing. They baked gingerbread and brewed root beer. Once Harriet made as many as 50 pies in an evening. Harriet and the former slaves used the proceeds from the sales to support themselves and to build a wash house where they could bathe and do laundry.

Slaves on this South Carolina plantation were declared free after the Union forces defeated the Confederate army.

Harriet had already put her life at risk many times to help runaway slaves. She would do the same during the Civil War in an effort to abolish slavery altogether. Just as she had used her cunning to rescue fugitives, she would employ it to serve as a scout and spy. By talking to African-Americans, she was able to obtain knowledge others could not. She could easily make her way into the black community by water or through the marsh. She recruited numerous black soldiers and gained information about the location of Confederate army camps as well as enemy tactics. Harkless Bowley, Harriet's grandnephew, noted that she was cautious and brave: "She penetrated the Rebel lines, told of their movements, and brought back other information of great value."

Almost 10 percent of the men in the Union army were African-American— one of them, an escaped slave, is shown here.

On January 1, 1863, both President Lincoln and Secretary of State William Seward signed the Emancipation Proclamation, a document formally freeing the slaves in the Confederacy. William's son Fred witnessed the official signing. The proclamation read in part: "And be it further enacted, that all slaves of persons who shall hereafter be engaged in rebellion against the government of the United States . . . shall be forever free of their servitude and not again held as slaves."

"I never, in my life, felt more certain that I was doing right, than I do in signing this paper," the president told his secretary of state. The proclamation was cause for great celebration among those who opposed slavery. Yet only the slaves in states that had seceded from the Union were declared free.

The Emancipation Proclamation freed slaves in the Confederate states.

Harriet was among those who thought President Lincoln had been too restrained: Freedom should be extended to all slaves.

In the spring of 1863, Union General David Hunter asked Harriet to lead a raid up the Combahee River in South Carolina—a first for a woman during the Civil War. Harriet agreed on the condition that she be joined by Colonel James Montgomery, who had fought with John Brown in Kansas and was then stationed near the river at Port Royal. Colonel Montgomery and Harriet made a good team. On June 1, they took 300 troops up the river in three boats. They set out at dawn as the fog rose over the rice fields. Along the way they stopped to allow the black soldiers to

Colonel James Montgomery, together with Harriet, led the raid up the Combahee River in South Carolina, freeing 800 slaves.

disembark. The men marched across the fields on a mission to recruit freed slaves to join the Union army.

The Union soldiers removed underwater mines so their boats could travel up the river. They set fire to plantation homes and destroyed stores of cotton and rice. Bridges and railroad tracks were taken out. African-American men, women, and children rushed from their cabins and across fields to find safety on the boats, bringing whatever they could carry, including pigs and chickens. The pigs squealed and the chickens squawked. All of them crowded onto the boats.

Harriet carried two pigs for a woman with a small child. When the order came to run, she tripped on her dress, tearing it to shreds. She vowed then never again to wear a long dress on an expedition and said she wanted a "bloomer" dress made of "coarse, strong material."

More passengers boarded the boats and Harriet's singing reassured them:

"Come from the East
Come from the West
Among all the glorious nations
This glorious one's the best.
Come along; come along; don't
be alarmed
For Uncle Sam is rich enough
To give you all a farm."

Abolitionist and women's suffrage leader Elizabeth Cady Stanton wears wide-legged pants called bloomers, a style made popular by Amelia Bloomer, also a women's rights advocate.

Sojourner Truth met with President Abraham Lincoln at the White House on October 29, 1864. She noted that he showed "kindness and consideration."

Eight hundred slaves were liberated on this mission. Out of this group, 100 joined the Union army.

Although some criticized the extensive destruction of property, others deemed the expedition successful and praised Harriet for her role. On July 17, 1863, Franklin Sanborn published a story in the *Boston Commonwealth*, an antislavery newspaper: "Col. Montgomery and his gallant band of 300 black soldiers, under the guidance of a black woman, dashed into the enemies' country, struck a bold and effective blow" and "brought off near 800 slaves and thousands of dollars worth of property, without losing a man or receiving a scratch."

"The good Lord has come down to deliver my people, and I must go and help him," Harriet told her friend Samuel May, a Unitarian minister. Samuel May later said, "She seemed to know no fear and scarcely ever fatigue." Harriet was more than willing to support the Union cause. Yet she had not been one of President Lincoln's early admirers, since she believed that early on he should have taken an even stronger stand to abolish slavery.

Over time, Harriet would change her opinion of Abraham Lincoln. When asked why she had never met the president,

Sojourner Truth
(1797–1883)

Sojourner Truth, tall, thin, serious-minded, bore little resemblance to Harriet Tubman. Born into slavery in Swartekill, New York, she remained a slave until the abolition of slavery in New York in 1827. Like Harriet, she was deeply religious and spoke out against slavery. Her most well-known speech was titled "Ain't I a Woman?" According to Samuel May, her words were "pertinent, impressive, and sometimes thrilling."

she answered, "I didn't like Lincoln in those days. I used to go see Mrs. Lincoln, but I never wanted to see him. . . . [We] didn't understand then [that] he was our friend." It was the abolitionist Sojourner Truth, a former slave and an ardent abolitionist and women's rights advocate, who would convince Harriet that Abraham Lincoln was indeed the friend of African-Americans. Sojourner Truth recalled a visit she had paid the president. After thanking him for all he had done, he "told her he had done nothing himself; he was only a servant of the country." Later Harriet admitted, "Yes, I am sorry now I didn't see Mr. Lincoln and thank him."

Sadly, an assassin's bullet would cut short the president's life in the final days of the war. Harriet would never meet Abraham Lincoln, but would join the country in mourning his death.

"The good Lord has come down to deliver my people, and I must go and help him."

–Harriet Tubman to Samuel May

chapter **10**

"Bind Up the Nation's Wounds"

"Fondly do we hope, fervently do we pray, that this mighty scourge of war may speedily pass away. . . . With malice toward none, with charity for all, with firmness in the right as God gives us to see the right, let us strive on to finish the work we are in, to bind up the nation's wounds, to care for him who shall have borne the battle and for his widow and his orphan, to do all which may achieve and cherish a just and lasting peace among ourselves and with all nations."

The clouds parted and the sun shone as President Abraham Lincoln, newly reelected, spoke these words on the occasion of his second inauguration. More than half the people who gathered outside the U.S. Capitol to hear his address on March 4, 1865, were African-American. Within weeks, the Confederate general Robert E. Lee surrendered to General Ulysses S. Grant at the Appomattox Court House in Virginia. The war was over. And with the war, slavery in the United States had come to an end.

On April 14, 1865, President Lincoln and his wife, Mary Todd Lincoln, attended a performance of *Our American Cousin* at Ford's Theatre in Washington, D.C.

John Wilkes Booth, a well-known actor who supported the Confederate cause and opposed the abolition of slavery, shot the president once in the back of the head and then fled the theater. At the same time, Lewis Paine, a Confederate soldier, entered William Seward's home and attacked him with a knife. William was seriously injured, but survived the attack.

John Wilkes Booth shot President Lincoln as the president watched a performance with Mary Todd Lincoln, Major Henry Rathbone, and Clara Harris. Major Rathbone was later wounded as he tried to grab Booth.

President Lincoln was carried across the street to the Petersen boarding house. He would die the next morning. As word of his assassination spread, the country suffered from shock and grief.

ASSASSINATION

Assassination is the planned murder of a prominent person.

The president's body was put on view in the White House. Mary Lincoln had already lost two sons—Edward in 1850 and

President Lincoln's funeral procession in New York City was a formal affair, complete with a horse-drawn carriage to transport the president's body.

Willie in 1862—and now she grieved all the more. On April 21, the bodies of the president and of his son Willie were placed on a railway car. The long train journey to Springfield, Illinois, Abraham Lincoln's hometown, began. At each stop, thousands of people came out to mourn their president, a leader devoted to binding up the nation's wounds, who had given his life to preserve the Union and end slavery.

Harriet traveled to Fort Monroe in Virginia, where she cared for the black soldiers who remained there, many

"A nobler, higher spirit, or a truer, seldom dwells in the human form."

–William Seward,
speaking of Harriet Tubman

of them sick or dying. Disturbed by the treatment of the African-American troops, she went to Washington to see William Seward for the first time since his attempted assassination. William had lost his wife Frances only weeks before Harriet's arrival. Harriet tried to comfort her friend and he, in turn, offered her advice, instructing her to talk to the surgeon general, Joseph Barnes, to see if hospital reforms could be made to make conditions better for black patients. Dr. Barnes promised to institute hospital reforms and also appointed Harriet the "matron" of the African-American hospital at Fort Monroe.

Concerned about supporting her family, Harriet wanted the government to pay her for her work as an army nurse and scout. She hoped that William Seward might be able to help. William wrote a letter to General David Hunter, explaining her situation and attesting to her character: "I have known her long, and a nobler, higher spirit, or a truer, seldom dwells in the human form. I commend her, therefore, to your kind and best attentions." Even this letter was not enough to produce results. Because she had never been given a formal appointment, Harriet would not be eligible for back pay. But she knew that had she been a

PENSION

A pension is a fixed sum of money paid to a person after he or she retires.

white male, she would have collected a government pension.

In October 1865, Harriet made plans to return to Auburn to care for her family. After arriving in Philadelphia, she was told that since she had worked as a nurse in an army hospital she could buy one of the half-fare train tickets to which soldiers were entitled. However, as she boarded the train the conductor looked at her ticket and told her that African-Americans had no right to use half-fare tickets. Harriet explained that she should have the same privileges as an army soldier. But the conductor did not listen. He grabbed her by the arm and shouted, "I'll make you tired of trying to stay here."

Harriet was prohibited from riding on a train car with white passengers.

The conductor attempted to throw Harriet out of the train car, but she resisted. Three men came to the conductor's aid and together they shoved Harriet into the baggage car.

Her arm and shoulder injured, Harriet arrived in New York City. As she left the train a young man approached her and gave her his card. He advised her to sue the conductor and offered to serve as a witness. Harriet was treated by a doctor

Martha Coffin Wright was a fervent abolitionist, and also taught painting and writing at a Quaker School.

in New York and then made the last leg of her journey, arriving home in Auburn. The pain in her shoulder lingered, and she had to keep her arm in a sling. Harriet consulted with Martha Wright and her husband, David, who encouraged her to file a suit. The card the young man had given Harriet had no address—only a name. Harriet, Martha, and David tried to locate him—even placing advertisements, but he was never found, and the suit did not go forward.

On December 18, 1865, Secretary of State William Seward made a public announcement that the Thirteenth Amendment to the Constitution had

SUE

A person who has been wronged may sue (or file a suit) to seek justice in a court of law.

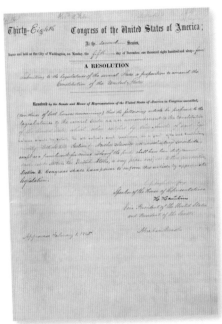

William Lloyd Garrison credited President Lincoln with the passage of the Thirteenth Amendment, which abolished slavery.

been adopted and that it had been ratified by 27 of the 36 states. This amendment abolished slavery throughout the nation and gave Congress the power to make laws to enforce the abolition. There was great rejoicing among the African-American and abolitionist communities.

Although the war was over, the battle for equal rights was not. Frances Ellen Watkins Harper, an African-American abolitionist and women's rights advocate, spoke at the meeting of the National Woman Suffrage Association in May 1866. She spoke of discrimination and described how she could not take a seat in a streetcar in Philadelphia or ride in the passenger car of a train between Washington and Baltimore. In the

"Neither slavery nor involuntary servitude . . . shall exist within the United States"

—Thirteenth Amendment to the U.S. Constitution

same speech she also referred to Harriet Tubman: "That woman who had led one of Montgomery's most successful expeditions, who was brave enough and secretive enough to act as a scout for the American army, had her hands all swollen from a conflict with a brutal conductor, who undertook to eject her from her place."

There would be many more reminders of unequal treatment and prejudice in the months and years ahead. In October 1867, Harriet learned that her husband John had been killed in a fight with a white man named Robert Vincent. There was one witness, John's 13-year-old son, but his testimony would be ignored. Robert Vincent was tried— and freed after a 10-minute deliberation by the jury.

Earning a living was hard work. Harriet took in boarders, tended the apple orchards, and grew her own vegetables. She set up fruit and vegetable stands on her

Frances Ellen Watkins Harper (1825–1911)

A contemporary of Harriet Tubman, fellow abolitionist Frances Ellen Watkins Harper was born to free parents in Baltimore, Maryland, and later moved to Ohio, where she was a teacher and poet and joined the American Anti-Slavery Society. She supported women's rights and gave public readings of her written works, including *Forest Leaves* and *Light Beyond the Darkness*.

property. She also went door to door carrying large baskets filled with fresh-grown produce. To make ends meet she often did domestic chores for Martha Wright.

Harriet was responsible for a large household that included her parents, Margaret Stewart, and friends and family members who had escaped from slavery. Harriet wanted to help clothe, feed, and educate them and also care for many of the newly freed people she had met during the war. She organized a fair to raise money and enlisted Martha Wright and others to make handicrafts, such as rag dolls, aprons, and bags. The proceeds were used to support two schools for African-Americans in South Carolina. In 1868, Harriet developed a new fundraising scheme. She would work with a writer on a book to tell the story of her life. Sarah Hopkins Bradford, an author of children's books who had written a story about a fugitive slave, agreed to take on the project. She lived in Geneva, New York, a few miles from Auburn, and had met Harriet while

Harriet posed for this formal portrait in the late 1860s in a photography studio in Auburn, New York.

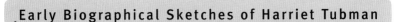

Early Biographical Sketches of Harriet Tubman

As a consequence of her enslavement, Harriet never learned to write. But others were eager to record her story: Abolitionist Franklin Sanborn (1831–1917) gathered material from interviews with Harriet and published the first short biography of Harriet Tubman on July 17, 1863, in the *Boston Commonwealth*. He hoped his writing would help solicit contributions that could be used to help support Harriet's work in South Carolina and provide care for her parents. Sanborn would later write biographies of several of his contemporaries, including Henry David Thoreau, John Brown, Bronson Alcott, and Nathaniel Hawthorne.

Ednah Dow Cheney (1824–1904) was born in Boston, and became a writer and reformer who was active in the New England Freedmen's Aid Society, an organization to help support newly freed slaves. She first met Harriet Tubman there in 1859. Over the course of several years, Ednah Cheney gathered information for an article titled "Moses" that would be published in 1865 in the *Freedmen's Record*. Like Franklin Sanborn's article, "Moses" would raise public awareness of Harriet Tubman and her work.

visiting her brother Samuel Hopkins, a professor at the Auburn Theological Seminary. Harriet visited Sarah in Geneva and talked with her at length. Sarah recorded her story and also solicited testimonials from well-known abolitionists, including Frederick Douglass, Thomas Garrett, Franklin Sanborn, William Seward, and Lucretia Mott.

The book *Scenes in the Life of Harriet Tubman* was published by the end of the year, and was made available at the Harriet Tubman Fair. Martha Wright's sister Lucretia Mott

Sarah Hopkins Bradford wrote short stories, biographies of Peter the Great and Christopher Columbus, a novel, and children's books before her biography of Harriet Tubman.

and her daughter Ellen, who had married the son of the abolitionist newspaper publisher William Lloyd Garrison, helped promote the book. Harriet collected $1,200 in proceeds. Sarah Bradford was later criticized for writing the book too hastily—she had plans to go to Europe and had rushed to finish. Important facts were left out and errors (such as the names of Harriet's enslavers) were made. Nevertheless, the book paid a well-deserved tribute to Harriet's heroism, comparing her to soldier and saint Joan of Arc and pioneering nurse Florence Nightingale.

One of Harriet's boarders was a war veteran named Nelson Davis. Although he was 20 years younger than Harriet, the two developed a deep friendship, and were married at the Central Presbyterian Church in Auburn. Many of Harriet's antislavery friends attended the wedding in the predominantly white church.

Nelson, a former slave, was born in Elizabeth City, North Carolina. He had enlisted in the army at Camp William Penn and fought at the Battle of Olustee in Florida. After he was discharged he moved to Auburn, renting a room in Harriet's home and working in the brickyard. Once they were married, Nelson and Harriet managed a brick-making business together. Nelson helped start the African Methodist Episcopal Zion Church, and was named a trustee in 1870. The church would become an important spiritual home and a social gathering place for both Harriet and Nelson.

For much of her life, Harriet had rarely stayed in one place for very long. As a child she had served several masters and slept under different roofs. After she escaped from slavery she made frequent trips on the Underground Railroad. While living in Canada and in Auburn, she often abandoned her home for a rescue mission or an antislavery convention. Once the Civil War started, she traveled from Boston to South Carolina to support the Union cause. Yet now, at the age of 47, Harriet would stay closer to home. Nelson, although a young man, was suffering from tuberculosis and Harriet needed to care for him.

Harriet and Nelson Davis worshipped at the African Methodist Episcopal Zion Church on Parker Street in Auburn. The church is still standing.

chapter **11**

Harriet Tubman
Home for the Aged

Harriet's good friend William Seward led an adventurous life—and his last years had been no exception. As secretary of state for President Andrew Johnson, he arranged for the purchase of Alaska from Russia—a decision ridiculed at the time and referred to as Seward's Folly. After he retired, William traveled around the world, visiting Alaska, the Middle East, India, Southeast Asia, Japan, and Hawaii. He died at home in Auburn on October 10, 1872.

William Seward signs the Alaska Treaty of Cessation on March 30, 1867. (He is seated to the left of the globe.)

After his death Harriet still owed money on her property and was able to pay William's son Frederick $1,200. On May 29, 1873, Frederick signed over the deed to Harriet. The property was now hers.

After the Civil War Confederate paper money lost its monetary worth, but Confederate gold was still valuable.

But Harriet's financial difficulties did not come to an end. Indeed, they would plague her the rest of her life.

In 1873, Harriet's brother John Stewart was approached by two men who told him that a newly freed slave from South Carolina had given them a trunk filled with Confederate gold worth $5,000 and wanted to exchange it for $2,500 in cash. John introduced the men to Harriet to see if she could help. After hearing their story, Harriet agreed to raise the cash. She found a local businessman named Anthony Shimer willing to put up the money. When Harriet told the men about Anthony, they asked her to hand over the money and promised to bring the gold later. Harriet refused and said she had to see the gold first. The men explained that the trunk of gold was hidden in the woods. That night they led her on a walk across the fields and into the woods. They found the trunk covered in leaves but could not open it. The men insisted Harriet give them the cash in exchange for the trunk. Once again she refused. Then the men told Harriet they would fetch the key and return.

When the men left, Harriet examined the trunk in the moonlight and found no keyhole. For the first time she became suspicious. She was searching for a rock she could use to break open the box, when she suddenly lost consciousness.

Harriet awoke to find herself bound and gagged—she could not remember what had happened. The cash she had brought with her was gone. She stumbled through the woods, lost and unable to find her way. Later that day her brother John and Anthony Shimer, the businessman, found her in the woods. Her clothing was torn, and her arms and legs were cut and bruised. Shimer's money was never returned, and Harriet's reputation suffered—but not by much. The people of Auburn understood that Harriet struggled financially

Harriet is on the left. Her husband, Nelson Davis, is seated to her right. Gertie Davis, their adopted daughter, stands between them. (This is the only existing photograph of Nelson Davis.)

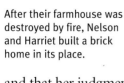

After their farmhouse was destroyed by fire, Nelson and Harriet built a brick home in its place.

and that her judgment in matters related to money was not always sound.

In 1874, Harriet and Nelson adopted a baby girl and called her Gertie. This daughter would grow up in a warm and caring environment. Although Harriet's father had died, her mother, Rit, still lived with them, as did four boarders who were treated like members of the family. Margaret Stewart was now married and living nearby.

The farmhouse, which Harriet had worked so hard to purchase, was destroyed in a fire on February 10, 1880. The family lost most of its belongings, including Harriet's prized collection of letters from abolitionists. But Nelson and Harriet soon rebuilt their home, using brick from the neighboring brickyard.

Harriet had often dreamed of starting a hospital for the aged. When the property next to hers—25 acres of land that included several buildings—was auctioned, Harriet was among the bidders. As the only nonwhite bidder, she felt out of her element. But with a bid of $1,450, she secured the property for her own. It was money she did not have, but was sure she could

Susan B. Anthony and Elizabeth Cady Stanton

Susan B. Anthony was born in Massachusetts and spent her childhood in Battenville, New York. Her father took her out of school and taught her at home after he learned she had not been receiving the same education as the boys. She worked as a teacher and a headmistress before moving to Rochester at the age of 29. She supported the abolitionist movement and became an active member of William Lloyd Garrison's American Anti-Slavery Society. After meeting reformer Elizabeth Cady Stanton, Anthony campaigned for women's rights as well. In 1869, the two women founded the National Women's Suffrage Association. They objected to the Fifteenth Amendment because it extended voting rights to African-American men, but not to women—black or white.

Susan B. Anthony

Elizabeth
Cady Stanton

raise. One of the buildings—a large, wood-frame, 10-room house—would become a residence for senior citizens.

Another building, this one made of brick, would be used as an infirmary for the aged and would be called the John Brown Hall. Harriet looked after the residents as well as the land, cultivating a garden where every spring irises, lilies, and lilacs bloomed.

To help with the cost, Harriet asked Sarah Bradford to write a new edition of her biography. In 1886, *Harriet, the Moses of Her People* was published. Once again Harriet started to make public appearances. She spoke at the Non-Partisan Society of Political Education for Women in Auburn. The local newspaper reported: "Her speech, though brief, was very interesting, and was listened to with rapt attention by all."

Meanwhile Nelson became increasingly ill with tuberculosis. He died in October 1888 and was buried at Fort Hill cemetery in Auburn. He was only 44 years old.

Harriet applied for a widow's pension from the government. It would take years for the application to be approved. In 1895, she was finally awarded $8 a month. Later, in 1899, she was granted an additional $12 a month for serving as a nurse to the Union Army—34 years after the end of the Civil War.

Without Nelson to look after, Harriet wandered farther afield to promote her causes. In July 1896, at the founding convention of the National Association of Colored

Harriet bought this building at an auction to use as a home for the aged.

Harriet is seated outside John Brown Hall. The building was used as an infirmary.

Women (NACW) in Washington, D.C., Harriet gave a speech entitled "More Homes for our Aged Ones." Still admired for her lovely singing voice, she sang a Civil War melody. By the time she left Washington, several audience members had pledged contributions to her Home for the Aged.

Even England's Queen Victoria wanted to pay tribute to the famous Underground Railroad conductor. In 1897, the year of her Diamond Jubilee, the 60th anniversary of her reign, she rewarded distinguished persons with silver medals bearing the image of the queen and her family. Queen Victoria read Harriet's life story and sent her one of the medals, as well as a lace shawl. These were treasures Harriet would prize for the rest of her life.

Harriet frequently spoke at the women's suffrage meetings in Rochester, New York, chaired by women's rights leaders Susan B. Anthony and Elizabeth Cady Stanton. At one meeting, when it came time for Harriet to speak, the audience could see that she

SUFFRAGE

Suffrage is the right to vote. Women were not granted this right in the United States until 1920.

was asleep. Harriet still drifted off at unpredictable moments. On this occasion, it became difficult to rouse her, but when she did wake up, she climbed onto the platform and, with her usual grace and a strong voice, spoke to the assembled crowd:

"Yes, ladies, I was the conductor of the Underground Railroad for eight years, and I can say what most conductors can't say—I never ran my train off the track and I never lost a passenger." The laughter and applause made it clear that she had charmed the crowd.

Harriet's health was deteriorating. Ever since she received the blow to her head as a child, she had experienced recurring pain, headaches, and disturbing visions. In 1901, she sought help from a surgeon in Boston. He performed an operation without giving her an anesthetic. "I just lay down like a lamb before the slaughter, and he sawed open my skull, and raised it up, and now it feels more comfortable," Harriet recalled. She got up, put on her bonnet, and started to walk home, but her legs were too weak. Although she had endured the surgery without an anesthetic, she would have to send for an ambulance to bring her home.

Maintaining the Home for the Aged proved to be more than Harriet could handle. In 1903, after running the institution for seven years, Harriet handed over the property to the African Methodist Episcopal Zion Church. Harriet would stay involved, but she relinquished her financial responsibility.

ANESTHETIC

An anesthetic, a drug that causes a lack of feeling, is given to patients undergoing surgery.

> *"I know God will raise up others to take care of the future."*
>
> –Harriet Tubman

In 1908, the Home for the Aged was renamed the Harriet Tubman Home. Fundraising had made renovations possible, so that older residents could live more comfortably. The dedication ceremony began with a parade that included a lively band and a procession of carriages. Harriet, "with the stars and stripes wound about her shoulders," rode in the first carriage and was accompanied by other prominent African-Americans, many of whom paid tribute to her. On June 23, 1908, the *Auburn Daily Advertiser* reported that the "aged Harriet Tubman Davis, the Moses of her people, yesterday experienced one of the happiest moments of her life." Harriet told the crowd, "I did not take up this work for my own benefit but for those of my race who need help. The work is now well started and I know God will raise up others to take care of the future. All I ask for is united effort, for 'united we stand: divided we fall.'"

Harriet, now in her mid-eighties, continued to devote more energy to her work than to her house. Martha Wright's daughter Ellen Wright Garrison dropped in on Harriet and found "quantities of old dry goods boxes (for kindling), old cooking utensils sitting on the ground, old wagons & an old buggy in rags and tatters." As usual, there was plenty of activity—two children eating apples, five cats, a dog and four puppies, a pig, and chickens. Harriet may have had trouble keeping up with her house, but she still enjoyed the company of her friends and neighbors. Evelyn Harris, a good friend, remembers visits to Harriet's home. Everyone called her "Aunt Harriet," even those who met her for the first time. Young and old enjoyed frequent sleigh rides, get-togethers, and cookouts.

Not until May 19, 1911, did Harriet move from her own house into the Harriet Tubman Home. She had spent many years looking after others while struggling to make ends meet; now she was ready to let others care for her. She had lost the use of her legs and spent much time in bed or in a wheelchair. Although physical tasks proved difficult, her mind stayed sharp. She could still tell stories and make people laugh. And, when speaking to visitors, she seized every opportunity to promote one of her causes.

Harriet spent the last weeks of her life in this room in the Harriet Tubman Home. The quilts were made by family members.

chapter 12
"United Effort"

During the winter of 1912, Harriet appeared frail and thin. She had always liked to talk, but now she was short of breath. As usual, she struggled to make ends meet. She spent what money she had not for her own nursing care, but to buy a cow to provide milk for the residents of the Harriet Tubman Home.

Harriet developed pneumonia, and must have had a premonition that she would die. On March 10, 1913, she asked her good friends—the clergy from the African Methodist Episcopal Zion Church and others— to participate in a final worship service. Despite her cough, Harriet

Even in old age, Harriet cared for her family, friends, and those in need.

joined in the singing. She died that day at the age of 91. Her grandniece (and Margaret Stewart's daughter) Alice Brickler later recalled: "It is said that on the day of her death, her strength returned to her. She arose from her bed with little assistance, ate heartily, walked about the rooms of the Old Ladies' Home which she liked so much and then went back to bed and

This photograph of Margaret Stewart Lucas with her daughter Alice was taken around 1900. Alice often said that her mother Margaret was Harriet's favorite niece.

her final rest. Whether this is true or not, it is typical of her. She believed in mind [over] matter. Regardless of how impossible a task might seem, if it were her task she tackled it with a determination to win."

Despite the hardships she endured, Harriet had not let herself feel despair. She had tremendous faith that helped sustain her. "I never met with any person of any color who had more confidence in the voice of God," Thomas Garrett, the Underground Railroad conductor, once said.

On March 13, prayers were offered at the Harriet Tubman Home. Harriet's body lay in state—she was dressed in black

Harriet used the proceeds from *Scenes in the Life of Harriet Tubman* to help fund her causes.

and wore the medal from Queen Victoria. The casket was draped with an American flag.

That afternoon, Harriet's body was taken to the A. M. E. Zion Church. There, hundreds of people attended a lengthy and elaborate service. Clergy from different churches spoke, and a quartet from the Central Presbyterian Church where Harriet and Nelson Davis were married sang two selections: "The Sands of Time Are Sinking" and "Good Night, I'm Going Home."

The head of the city council, Jaeckel Spoke, paid tribute to Harriet: "I may say that I have known 'Aunt Harriet' during my whole lifetime. The boys of my time always regarded her as a sort of supernatural being; our youthful imaginations were fired by the tales we had heard of her adventures and we stood in great awe of her. In later years I came to know her more intimately. . . .

> *"Our youthful imaginations were fired by the tales we had heard of her adventures."*
>
> –Jaeckel Spoke of the Auburn city council, at Harriet's memorial

She was a woman of unusual judgment and great common sense." Jaeckel Spoke believed that greatness in life did not come by accident. Harriet owed hers to "great zeal accompanied by great faith in the object sought," as well as "the persistent fighting against great obstacles."

W. E. B. DuBois, the civil rights activist and author, recognized the sacrifices Harriet Tubman had made for her race and later that month wrote: "Harriet Tubman fought American slavery single handed and was a pioneer in that organized effort known as the Underground Railroad."

W. E. B. DuBois (1868–1963)

W. E. B. DuBois was a civil rights activist, historian, editor and prolific writer. He was born in Great Barrington, Massachusetts, and studied at Fisk University in Nashville, Tennessee; Harvard University; and the University of Berlin. After traveling in Europe, he returned to Harvard where he earned his PhD—the first African-American to do so.

Throughout the year Harriet would continue to be remembered for her generosity of spirit. On June 12, 1914, the citizens of Auburn honored her with a memorial tablet. The mayor made a formal presentation at the Auditorium Theater. The hall went dark and only the little red, white, and blue lights framing the tablet were left shining. After Alice Brickler removed the American flag that covered the tablet, Dr. Booker T. Washington gave an oration. He praised Harriet Tubman's great contributions and called her "one of the best educated persons that ever lived in this country," despite her lack of formal schooling.

Following the ceremony, the guests celebrated until the early hours of the morning. It was reported that "new steps were danced by the younger people while the older folks enjoyed the old steps. . . . The hall presented a brilliant appearance with the tasty decorations and the beautiful dresses of the ladies."

Booker T. Washington (1856–1915)

Booker T. Washington was born a slave in Hale's Ford, Virginia. He became a free man in 1865. A famed orator and author of *Up From Slavery,* he was a forceful proponent of education for African-Americans. In 1881, he founded the Tuskegee Institute in Alabama, a black college. Although he always promoted the rights of African-Americans, he was sometimes criticized for being too accommodating to whites.

The bronze tablet was moved to the Cayuga County Courthouse, where it remains today. It reads in part:

Called the "Moses" of her people during the Civil War, with rare courage, she led over three hundred Negroes up from slavery to freedom, and rendered invaluable service as nurse and spy.

In the years to come, however, Harriet Tubman's reputation would suffer. Her legacy was ignored and her memory started to fade. Little information about her life was

The ceremony to unveil this plaque in Harriet's honor was attended by the mayor of Auburn, Booker T. Washington, Civil War veterans, and many others.

recorded. In 1932, children's book author Hildegarde Hoyt Swift was the first to publish an account. She included a fictionalized story of Harriet Tubman's life in *The Railroad to Freedom: A Story of the Civil War.*

Three African-American artists helped to assure Harriet's place in history. In 1931, Harlem

"With implicit trust in God, she braved every danger and overcame every obstacle."

–from the Harriet Tubman plaque

Harriet Tubman by William H. Johnson

William H. Johnson painted this portrait of Harriet Tubman around 1945. The depiction of Harriet bearing a gun has been controversial. The gun is seen by some as a symbol of power. However, other historians and educators would prefer Harriet to be portrayed without a gun. They argue that although Harriet may have on occasion carried a gun, she is not known to have used one. To them, Harriet's intelligence, wit, and cunning accounted for her success.

Renaissance painter Aaron Douglass depicted a newly freed woman, raising her arms high above her head, her hands clasping broken chains, in *Spirits Rising,* also called the Harriet Tubman mural. Jacob Lawrence celebrated Harriet's life journey in a series of 31 paintings he started in 1939. Thirty years later he continued to pay tribute to Harriet by illustrating a picture book titled *Harriet and the Promised Land.* William Johnson, an artist born in Florence, South Carolina, painted Harriet Tubman in the mid-1940s. He placed the North Star in the sky and dressed his American hero in a red-and-white striped skirt.

In 1938, Earl Conrad, a journalist from Auburn, began writing a biography of Harriet for adults. He remembered,

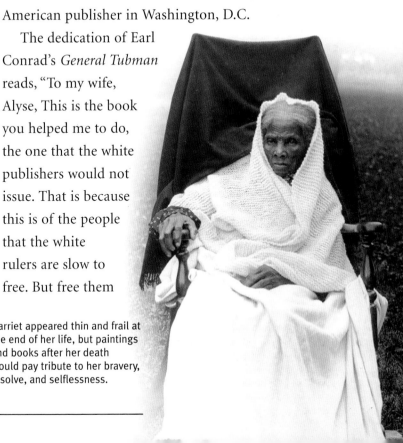

as a young boy, seeing Harriet Tubman seated on her front porch—the white shawl given to her by Queen Victoria draped around her shoulders. Earl Conrad did extensive research and interviewed friends and family, including Alice Lucas Brickler (Harriet's grandniece) and Harkless Bowley (her grandnephew). But it proved difficult to capture the interest of a major New York publishing company. However, in 1942, Carter Woodson, historian and publisher of the *Journal of Negro History,* offered Earl Conrad a contract from Associated Publishers, an African-American publisher in Washington, D.C.

The dedication of Earl Conrad's *General Tubman* reads, "To my wife, Alyse, This is the book you helped me to do, the one that the white publishers would not issue. That is because this is of the people that the white rulers are slow to free. But free them

Harriet appeared thin and frail at the end of her life, but paintings and books after her death would pay tribute to her bravery, resolve, and selflessness.

> *"Harriet Tubman lived to see the harvest."*
>
> —Langston Hughes

they must or conflicts like the present will go on until this matter is settled right."

Still, historians paid little attention to Harriet Tubman throughout the 20th century. However, several children's books kept her story alive: Dorothy Sterling's *Freedom Train* in 1954, Ann Petry's *Harriet Tubman* in 1955, and Ann McGovern's *Runaway Slave: The Story of Harriet Tubman* in 1965.

The African-American poet Langston Hughes told the story of Harriet Tubman's life in a children's book. He says that Harriet once asked a reporter for the *New York Herald* if he liked apples. The reporter answered "Yes." When she asked if he had ever planted apples, he said, "No." Harriet replied, "But somebody else planted them. I liked apples when I was young and I said, 'Some day I'll plant apples myself for other young folks to eat.' And I guess I did." Langston Hughes wrote, "Her apples were the apples of freedom. Harriet Tubman lived to see the harvest."

In 2003, several scholars started to pay attention to Harriet Tubman. Three biographers, Jean Humez, Kate Clifford Larson, and Catherine Clinton, made an effort to give a fair representation without exaggerating Harriet Tubman's achievements. They wanted to set the record straight. Each author uncovered new material and shed light on historical facts. Kate Clifford Larson, for example, determined that

Harriet's birthplace was not in Bucktown, but most probably in Harrisville, on Anthony Thompson's property.

The three authors believed that Harriet Tubman was one of America's greatest heroes. Yet they wanted to demythologize Harriet and show her human qualities, her flaws, as well as her strengths. They attempted to provide an accurate accounting of the number of rescue missions—10 to 13, not the 19 Sarah Bradford and Harriet's other contemporary biographers had recorded. They recalculated the number of slaves Harriet had liberated: The new count is between 70 and 80, not 300 as is stated on historical markers. (Harriet may also have given information on escape routes and instructions to an additional 50 or 60 slaves.)

The country's leaders are proud of the role Harriet Tubman played in history. In his commencement address to Arizona State University on May 14, 2009, President Barack Obama referred to Harriet Tubman. He mentioned "a willingness to question conventional wisdom and rethink old dogmas; a lack of regard for all

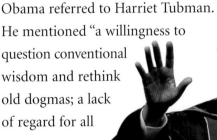

President Barack Obama encourages young people to be daring and question conventional wisdom just as Harriet did.

"Regardless of how impossible a task might seem . . . she tackled it with a determination to win."

–Harriet's grandniece Alice Brickler

the traditional markers of status and prestige— and a commitment instead to doing what's meaningful to you, what helps others, what makes a difference in this world." It was this "quality of mind and quality of heart," he said, that "inspired a 30-year-old escaped slave to run an underground railroad to freedom."

Recalling her childhood, Harriet Tubman said, "I grew up like a neglected weed, ignorant of liberty, having no experience of it. Then I was not happy or contented: every time I saw a white man I was afraid of being carried away." William Wells Brown reminds us that "her back and shoulders, marked with the biting lash, told how inhuman was the institution from which she had fled." Harriet would run away from those who had oppressed her. It was a difficult and dangerous journey. But Harriet was, as Ednah Cheney noted in 1865, "profoundly practical and highly imaginative." The strength of her character would make her escape possible.

As she traveled the Underground Railroad, Harriet connected with people and formed deep friendships— with fugitive slaves, with the great antislavery leaders, with her friends and neighbors. After achieving freedom for herself, her love for her family and her willingness to help others drove her to take great risks, making it possible for her to lead African-Americans out of captivity. Later in life, she stood up for people whose rights were denied, and she would not stop caring for those in need.

Harriet never learned to read or write, but she had a prodigious memory, a big heart, and courage. She became a master storyteller whose words made people aware of the evils of slavery and the struggles African-Americans endured to win their freedom. Her speeches advanced the abolitionist cause and helped extend rights to African-Americans and to women. Harriet Tubman's passion, her wit, her charm, and the wealth of her experience gave power to her voice. It is a voice that changed history—and one that still needs to be heard.

Monuments to Harriet Tubman have been erected around the world—from New York to Ghana. The Harriet Tubman Memorial in Boston's South End shows the Moses of her people, larger than life, leading a group of fugitives to freedom.

Events in the Life of Harriet Tubman

c. 1834–1836
An overseer hits Harriet on the head with an iron weight. The injury will have lifelong consequences.

February or March 1822
Araminta Ross (later known as Harriet Tubman) is born on Anthony Thompson's farm on the Eastern Shore of Maryland.

Fall 1849
Harriet escapes from slavery and finds refuge in Philadelphia.

December 1850
Harriet returns to Maryland to rescue her niece Kessiah and Kessiah's two children.

June 1857
Harriet brings her parents to Canada.

October 1859
John Brown is captured after leading a raid on the armory at Harpers Ferry.

c. 1844
Harriet marries John Tubman, a free African-American.

c. 1829
Harriet is hired out to work for James Cook.

THREE HUNDRED DOLLARS REWARD.

RANAWAY from the subscriber on Monday the 17th ult., three negroes, named as follows: HARRY, aged about 19 years, has on one side of his neck a wen, just under the ear, he is of a dark chestnut color, about 5 feet 8 or 9 inches hight; BEN, aged aged about 25 years, is very quick to speak when spoken to, he is of a chestnut color, about six feet high; MINTY, aged about 27 years, is of a chestnut color, fine looking, and about 5 feet high. One hundred dollars reward will be given for each of the above named negroes, if taken out of the State, and $50 each if taken in the State. They must be lodged in Baltimore, Easton or Cambridge Jail, in Maryland.

ELIZA ANN BRODESS,
Near Buckown, Dorchester county, Md.
Oct. 3d, 1849.

Christmas 1854
Harriet takes her three brothers to St. Catharines in Ontario, Canada.

1850
The Fugitive Slave Act makes it legal to capture former slaves who have escaped to free states.

Spring 1859
Harriet purchases a home in Auburn, New York, with the help of William H. Seward.

May 1860
Harriet gives a speech at the New England Anti-Slavery Society Conference in Boston.

April 12, 1861
The first shots of the Civil War are fired at Fort Sumter, South Carolina.

1869
Scenes in the Life of Harriet Tubman by Sarah H. Bradford is published.

June 1886
Harriet purchases a 25-acre property on which she will establish a home for the aged.

January 1862
Massachusetts Governor John Andrew sends Harriet to South Carolina to work as a scout and nurse for the Union cause.

March 18, 1869
Harriet marries Nelson Davis, a war veteran.

June 1, 1863
Harriet helps lead the Combahee River raid in South Carolina.

November 1896
Harriet speaks at the New York Suffrage Convention in Rochester.

April 14, 1865
President Abraham Lincoln receives a fatal gunshot wound at Ford's Theatre.

March 10, 1913
Harriet dies of pneumonia at her Home for the Aged in Auburn, New York.

January 1, 1863
President Abraham Lincoln and Secretary of State William Seward sign the Emancipation Proclamation.

Bibliography

Barry, Joseph. *The Strange Story of Harper's Ferry with Legends of the Surrounding Country.* Martinsburg, West Virginia: Thompson Brothers, 1903.

Blockson, Charles L. *Hippocrene Guide to the Underground Railroad.* New York: Hippocrene Books, 1994.

Bordewich, Fergus M. *Bound For Canaan: The Underground Railroad and the War for the Soul of America.* New York: Amistad, 2006.

Bradford, Sarah H. *Harriet, The Moses of Her People.* New York: J.J. Little & Co., 1901.

_____. *Harriet Tubman: The Moses of Her People.* Bedford, Massachusetts: Applewood Press, 1993, first published 1886.

_____. *Scenes in the Life of Harriet Tubman.* Auburn: W.J. Moses, Printer, 1869.

Brown, William Wells. *The Rising Son; or, The Antecedents and Advancement of the Colored Race.* Boston: A.G. Brown & Co., 1874, reprinted by Mnemosyne Publishing Inc., 1969.

Cheney, Ednah Dow. "Moses." *Freedmen's Record,* March 1865. pp. 34–38.

Clinton, Catherine. *Harriet Tubman: The Road to Freedom.* Boston: Little, Brown and Company, 2004.

Conrad, Earl. *Harriet Tubman.* Washington, DC: Associated Publishers, 1943.

Douglas, Aaron. "The Aaron Douglas Fresco of Harriet Tubman." *The Crisis,* v. 9. January 1932. p. 449.

Douglass, Frederick. *Narrative of the Life of Frederick Douglass, an American Slave, Written by Himself.* Boston: Anti-Slavery Office, 1845.

Drew, Benjamin. *A North-Side View of Slavery. The Refugee: or the Narratives of Fugitive Slaves in Canada.* Boston: J. P. Jewett and Company, 1856, reprinted by Negro Universities Press, 1968.

Goodwin, Doris Kearns. *Team of Rivals: The Political Genius of Abraham Lincoln.* New York: Simon & Schuster, 2005.

Griffin, Fred G. "Toronto Minister the Son of a Slave Knew 'Uncle Tom', Saw Exodus to Canada." *The Toronto Star Weekly,* January 19, 1924.

Holt, Rosa Belle. "A Heroine in Ebony." *The Chautauquan: A weekly newsmagazine.* July 1896.

Hughes, Langston. *Famous American Negroes.* New York: Dodd Mead, 1954.

Humez, Jean M. *Harriet Tubman: The Life and the Life Stories.* Madison, WI: The University of Wisconsin Press, 2003.

King, Wilma. *Stolen Childhood: Slave Youth in Nineteenth-Century America.* Bloomington, IN: Indiana University Press, 1995.

Larson, Kate Clifford. *Bound for the Promised Land: Harriet Tubman, Portrait of an American Hero.* New York: Random House, 2004.

Lowry, Beverly. *Harriet Tubman: Imagining a Life.* New York: Random House, 2007.

Marks, Carole C. *Moses and the Monster and Miss Anne.* Urbana and Chicago: University of Illinois Press, 2009.

May, Samuel J. *Some Recollections of Our Antislavery Conflict.* Boston: Fields, Osgood, & Co., 1869.

Obama, Barack. "Remarks by the President at Arizona State University Commencement." May 14, 2009. http://www.whitehouse.gov/the_press_office/Remarks-By-The-President-At-Arizona-State-University-Commencement/

Petry, Ann. *Harriet Tubman: Conductor on the Underground Railroad.* New York: Simon & Schuster, 1955.

Sawyer, Kem Knapp. *Lucretia Mott: Friend of Justice.* Carlisle, MA: History Compass, 1998.

_____. *The Underground Railroad in American History.* Berkeley Heights, NJ: Enslow Publishers, 1997.

Sernett, Milton C. *Harriet Tubman: Myth, Memory, and History.* Durham, NC: Duke University Press, 2007.

Siebert, Wilbur H. *The Underground Railroad from Slavery to Freedom.* New York: The Macmillan Company, 1898.

Sterling, Dorothy. *Freedom Train: The Story of Harriet Tubman.* New York: Doubleday, 1954.

Still, William. *The Underground Railroad: Authentic Narratives and First-Hand Accounts.* Philadelphia: Porter & Coales, Publishers, 1872.

Stowe, Harriet Beecher. *Uncle Tom's Cabin.* Boston: John P. Jewett & Company, 1852.

Telford, Emma P. "Harriet: The Modern Moses of Heroism and Visions." *Typescript,* c. 1905. Cayuga Museum of History and Art.

Underground Railroad. Division of Publications, National Park Service, 1998.

Wheat, Ellen Harkins. *Jacob Lawrence: The Frederick Douglass and Harriet Tubman Series of 1938–40.* Hampton University Museum, 1991.

Works Cited

A few of the quotations recorded in dialect have been changed to reflect modern standard English.

pp. 8–9: "I'm on the way…" Bradford, *Harriet*, 49–50; p. 27: "I was always…" Tatlock, 7; p. 29: "flying over fields and towns…" Sanborn in Bradford, *Scenes*, 79; p. 35: "Every time I saw…" Drew, 30; p. 38: "I'll meet you in the morning." Bradford, *Scenes*, 18; p. 39: "I had reasoned this out in my mind…" Bradford, *Harriet*, 29; p. 41: "When I found I had crossed that line…" Bradford, *Scenes*, 19; p. 41: "a stranger in a strange land." Bradford, *Scenes*, 20; p. 42: "I would make a home…" Bradford, *Harriet*, 32; p. 43: "He gave me strength…" Cheney, 37; p. 46: "make all the trouble she could…" and "how foolish it was…" Cheney, 35; p. 47: "Several times she was…" Telford, 9; p. 48: "Oh go down, Moses…" Bradford, *Harriet*, 37; p. 49: "the deliverer of her people." Cheney, 35; p. 50: "The idea of being captured…never known before or since." Still, 306; p. 51: "A live runaway…" Still, 306; p. 52: "Read my letter…nor tail of it." Bradford, *Harriet*, 62–64; p. 57: "I wouldn't trust Uncle Sam…" Bradford, *Scenes*, 27; p. 64: "Yes, and the woman herself felt that she had the charm…" Brown, 538; p. 65: "Harriet Tubman will go…" Griffin, *Toronto Star Weekly*, 19 Jan. 1924.; p. 65: "No fugitive ever captured…" Brown, 537; p. 68: "I have seen hundreds of escaped slaves…" Drew, 30; p. 70: "I was beaten…" Drew, 42; p. 70: "I bring you…" Garrison, April 13, 1897, in Humez, 265; p. 71: "She has great dramatic power…" Cheney, 36–37; p. 76: "He did more in dying…" Wright, 10 Jan. 1869, in Humez, 40; p. 78: "She told the story…" "Woman's Rights Meetings," 1860, in Humez, 41; p. 81: "My people are free… you'll see it soon." Bradford, *Harriet*, 93; p. 83: "She penetrated…" Harkless Bowley, 8 Aug. 1939, in Humez, 247; p. 84: "I never, in my life, felt more certain…" Goodwin, 499; p. 85: "made of some coarse, strong material." Bradford, *Scenes*, 85; p. 85: "Come from the East…" Telford, 19; p. 86: "Col. Montgomery…receiving a scratch." in Humez, 58; p. 86: "The good Lord…" May, 406; p. 87: "I didn't like Lincoln…" Holt, 462; p. 87: "pertinent, impressive…" May, 406; p. 91: "I have known her long…" Bradford, *Scenes*, 65; p. 92: "I'll make you tired of trying to stay here." Bradford, *Scenes*, 46; p. 95: "That woman who had led…" "Proceedings of the Eleventh Women's Rights Convention" (1866) in Humez, 73; pp. 104–105: "her speech, though brief…" *Auburn Morning Dispatch*, 15 Mar. 1888, in Humez, 315; p. 107: "Yes, ladies, I was the conductor…" Bradford, Harriet 1901 edition, 142; p. 107: "I just lay down…" Bradford, Harriet 1901 edition, 151–2; p. 108: "aged Harriet Tubman Davis…divided we fall." *Auburn Citizen*, 24 Jun. 1908, in Humez, 106; p. 108: "quantities of old…." Ellen Wright Garrison, 22 Oct. 1906, in Humez, 323; p. 111: "It is said that on the day of her death…" Alice Lucas Bricker, 28 Jul. 1939, in Humez, 268; p. 111: "I never met…" Garrett in Bradford, *Scenes*, 49; p. 112: "I may say…great obstacles." *Auburn Daily Advertiser*, 13 Mar. 1913, in Humez, 329–330; p. 113: "Harriet Tubman fought…." *The Crisis*, March 1913, in Humez, 123 ; p. 114: "one of the best educated…" *Auburn Advertiser Journal*, 13 Jun. 1914, in Humez, 336; p. 114: "new steps… beautiful dresses of the ladies." *Auburn Advertiser Journal*, 13 Jun. 1914, in Humez, 336; p. 117: "To my wife, Alyse…" dedication by Earl Conrad in *General Tubman*; p. 118: "But somebody else planted them" Langston Hughes, 41–2.; p. 119: "a willingness to question…quality of heart…" Barack Obama; p. 120: "I grew up like a neglected weed…" Benjamin Drew, *A North-Side View of Slavery*, 30; p. 120: "profoundly practical and highly imaginative." Cheney, 35; p. 120: "Her back and shoulders…" Brown, 537.

For Further Study

Travel to Maryland's Eastern Shore and see the Harriet Tubman marker on the site of the Brodess plantation in Bucktown, Dorchester County. Plans are underway to erect a new birthplace marker in the Peters Neck district on the property that once belonged to Anthony Thompson. Contact the Harriet Tubman Museum in Cambridge, Maryland, for more information (410-228-0401).

Visit the Harriet Tubman Home (www.harriethouse.org) and the Seward House Museum (www.sewardhouse.org) in Auburn, New York. While there, you can also see the Harriet Tubman marker outside the courthouse, the A.M.E. Zion Church, and the Fort Hill Cemetery where Harriet Tubman, William Seward, and their families are buried.

Follow the path the fugitive slaves took through New York State, to Niagara Falls, and on to St. Catharines. Information on the Underground Railroad is available at the St. Catharines Museum (www.stcatharineslock3museum.ca).

For a history of the Harriet Tubman Home and the story of her life, see: www.nyhistory.com/harriettubman/

For information on the Underground Railroad see the website for the National Underground Railroad Freedom Center in Cincinnati, Ohio: www.freedomcenter.org

Index

Acknowledgments

I would like to thank all those who helped me with the research for this book: Donald Pender at the Harriet Tubman Museum in Cambridge, Maryland; Christine Carter at the Harriet Tubman Home in Auburn, New York; Pauline Copes-Johnson, Harriet Tubman's great grandniece, who shared many stories; Peter Wisbey at the Seward House Museum; Lynn Palmieri at the Cayuga Museum of History and Art; Arden Phair, curator at the St. Catharines Museum; and Sonia Forry at the Cape May Historical Museum. I am also grateful to several authors I have never met, but who have kept Harriet Tubman's story alive: Catherine Clinton, Jean Humez, Kate Clifford Larson, and Milton Sernett. Many thanks to Dr. Ida Jones at the Moorland-Spingarn Research Center at Howard University for careful reading and recommendations, to Anne Burns for her photo research, to Mark Johnson Davies for the design, and to John Searcy for making this a better book. Special thanks to Beth Hester, a terrific editor. As always my family provided much encouragement. Jon, Kate and Brian, Eve and Dan, and Ida, I can't thank you enough! Also my four grandchildren for all the joy they bring: Karenna, Jack, Raya, and Thomas!

Picture Credits

Front Cover Photo by Alamy Images/North Wind Picture Archive

Back Cover Photo by Maryland Historic Society

The photographs in this book are used with permission and through the courtesy of:

University of North Carolina at Chapel Hill Libraries: p.1. **Ohio Historical Society:** pp.2, 45, 56, 58, 62B, 63, 68. **Getty Images:** pp.4–5, 11B, 62T, 64, 81, 101, 102, 123TL; p.54 Willard Clay; p.69 National Geographic; p.119 AFP. **Library of Congress:** pp.6, 7, 8, 10, 11T, 13, 14, 16, 25, 27, 31, 38, 40, 48, 66, 67, 70, 76, 77, 80, 84T, 85, 86, 89, 90, 95, 104T, 117, 122TR&BC, 123BL, BC&BR. **Mary Konchar:** pp.12, 22, 23, 26. **Maryland Historic Society:** pp.17, 18, 33, 47. **Corbis:** p.19 John Baker; p.28 Medford Historic Society; pp.34, 55 Bettman; p.48 Swim Ink2, LLC; p.59, 104 Corbis; p.61 Albright-Knox Art Gallery. **Dorchester County Historical Society:** pp.20, 21. **DK Images:** pp.24, 32, 52. **Bridgeman Art Library:** p.30 New York Historical Society; p.49 Newberry Library; pp.53, 92 Private Collection; p.71 Newberry Library; p.79 Dreweatt Neate Fine Art Auctioneers. **The Cambridge Democrat:** pp.36, 44, 122BL. **North Wind Picture Archives:** pp.41, 72. **Library Company of Philadelphia:** p.42. **Cape May County Historical and Genealogical Society:** pp.43, 122TL. **Cayuga Museum of History and Art:** pp.57, 110. **Alamy Images:** p.39 National Geographic Image Collection; p.60 Jim West; p.83 London Art Archive; p.96 North Wind Picture Archive. **Boston Public Library:** p.78. **Kansas State Historical Society:** p.84B. **Bryn Mawr College:** p.93. **National Archives:** p.94. **Cayuga County Historian's Office:** p.99. **Seward House:** p.100. **Harriet Tubman Home:** pp.103, 105, 123TR. **The Image Works:** p.109 Stanley Walker/Syracruse Newspaper. **Duke University Rare Book & Manuscript Collection:** pp.112, 123TC. **Ambient Images:** p.115. **Art Resource:** p.116 Smithsonian American Art Museum. **SuperStock:** p.121 age footstock.

BORDER IMAGES, from left to right: Library of Congress, Library of Congress, Library of Congress, Cambridge Democrat, Library of Congress.

About the Author

Kem Knapp Sawyer was born in New York City. A graduate of Yale University, she has taught English and drama and directed plays for children. She lives in Washington, D.C., with her husband, journalist Jon Sawyer. Author of DK Biographies *Anne Frank, Eleanor Roosevelt,* and *Abigail Adams,* Kem enjoys writing for and talking to young people. Her books *The Underground Railroad in American History, Lucretia Mott: Friend of Justice,* and *Freedom Calls: Journey of a Slave Girl* will be of special interest to readers of *Harriet Tubman.* See kemsawyer.com for more.

Other DK Biographies you'll enjoy:

Abigail Adams
Kem Knapp Sawyer
ISBN 978-0-7566-5209-8 paperback
ISBN 978-0-7566-5208-1 hardcover

Marie Curie
Vicki Cobb
ISBN 978-0-7566-3831-3 paperback
ISBN 978-0-7566-3832-0 hardcover

Charles Darwin
David C. King
ISBN 978-0-7566-2554-2 paperback
ISBN 978-0-7566-2555-9 hardcover

Princess Diana
Joanne Mattern
ISBN 978-0-7566-1614-4 paperback
ISBN 978-0-7566-1613-7 hardcover

Amelia Earhart
Tanya Lee Stone
ISBN 978-0-7566-2552-8 paperback
ISBN 978-0-7566-2553-5 hardcover

Thomas Edison
Jan Adkins
ISBN 978-0-7566-5207-4 paperback
ISBN 978-0-7566-5206-7 hardcover

Albert Einstein
Frieda Wishinsky
ISBN 978-0-7566-1247-4 paperback
ISBN 978-0-7566-1248-1 hardcover

Benjamin Franklin
Stephen Krensky
ISBN 978-0-7566-3528-2 paperback
ISBN 978-0-7566-3529-9 hardcover

Gandhi
Amy Pastan
ISBN 978-0-7566-2111-7 paperback
ISBN 978-0-7566-2112-4 hardcover

Harry Houdini
Vicki Cobb
ISBN 978-0-7566-1245-0 paperback
ISBN 978-0-7566-1246-7 hardcover

Thomas Jefferson
Jacqueline Ching
ISBN 978-0-7566-4506-9 paperback
ISBN 978-0-7566-4505-2 hardcover

Helen Keller
Leslie Garrett
ISBN 978-0-7566-0339-7 paperback
ISBN 978-0-7566-0488-2 hardcover

Joan of Arc
Kathleen Kudlinksi
ISBN 978-0-7566-3526-8 paperback
ISBN 978-0-7566-3527-5 hardcover

John F. Kennedy
Howard S. Kaplan
ISBN 978-0-7566-0340-3 paperback
ISBN 978-0-7566-0489-9 hardcover

Martin Luther King, Jr.
Amy Pastan
ISBN 978-0-7566-0342-7 paperback
ISBN 978-0-7566-0491-2 hardcover

Abraham Lincoln
Tanya Lee Stone
ISBN 978-0-7566-0834-7 paperback
ISBN 978-0-7566-0833-0 hardcover

Nelson Mandela
Lenny Hort & Laaren Brown
ISBN 978-0-7566-2109-4 paperback
ISBN 978-0-7566-2110-0 hardcover

Mother Teresa
Maya Gold
ISBN 978-0-7566-3880-1 paperback
ISBN 978-0-7566-3881-8 hardcover

Annie Oakley
Chuck Wills
ISBN 978-0-7566-2997-7 paperback
ISBN 978-0-7566-2986-1 hardcover

Pelé
Jim Buckley
ISBN 978-0-7566-2987-8 paperback
ISBN 978-0-7566-2996-0 hardcover

Eleanor Roosevelt
Kem Knapp Sawyer
ISBN 978-0-7566-1496-6 paperback
ISBN 978-0-7566-1495-9 hardcover

Barack Obama
Stephen Krensky
ISBN 978-0-7566-5805-2 paperback
ISBN 978-0-7566-5804-5 hardcover

George Washington
Lenny Hort
ISBN 978-0-7566-0835-4 paperback
ISBN 978-0-7566-0832-3 hardcover

Laura Ingalls Wilder
Tanya Lee Stone
ISBN 978-0-7566-4508-3 paperback
ISBN 978-0-7566-4507-6 hardcover

31901046923258